The Christopher Nolan Method

The film studies primer for filmmakers and movie buffs

...

Table of Contents

Chapter 1: Introduction to Christopher Nolan

Overview of Nolan's filmography. 8

Brief biography of early life. 11

His influences: From Kubrick to Bond. 13

Early career and breakthrough with "Following" and "Memento." 16

His place in modern cinema. 20

Chapter 2: Storytelling and Narrative Structure

His idea creation method. 23

Writing process and schedule. 26

Analysis of the art of misdirection: Plot twists and reveals in "The Prestige" and "Inception." 28

Analysis of non-linear storytelling in "Memento," "Inception," and "Dunkirk." 31

Creating believable worlds: "Inception" and "Interstellar." 34

The rule of realism: Grounding the extraordinary 38

Chapter 3: The Psychological Depth: Characters and Themes

The recurring themes and motifs across his films...41

Identity and memory: Dissecting "Memento" and "The Prestige." 44

Morality and redemption: Character arcs in "The Dark Knight Trilogy." 47

Obsession and sacrifice: The human element in "Interstellar" and "Inception." 50

Complex villains: The Joker, Bane, and beyond. 53

The antagonist's purpose: Driving the narrative forward. 56

Chapter 4: Pre-production Essentials

Storyboarding: Nolan's approach to visualizing scenes. 60

Planning and research: The role of meticulous pre-production in Nolan's films. 63

Casting: Strategies behind choosing the right actors for character-driven storytelling. 66

Analysis of set design and location choice in establishing mood and theme. 69

Chapter 5: Nolan's Directing Techniques

In-Camera magic: The philosophy behind practical effects. 72

Integrating CGI with practical effects: Maintaining authenticity. 75

Nolan's unique approaches to directing, including his hands-on style and rehearsals. 78

Techniques Nolan uses to guide performances and create iconic performances. 81

Nolan's approach to visual composition and movement within a scene. 84

The integration of blocking with storytelling to enhance narrative impact. 87

Detailed scene analysis: Exploring the staging of key scenes in Nolan's films. 91

Chapter 6: Visual Style and Cinematography

Examination of Nolan's visual signature. 96

His use of long takes and tracking shots. 99

Use of IMAX to achieve visual grandeur. 102

Lighting and color: Techniques to create mood and focus. 105

Natural vs. artificial lighting in Nolan's films. 108

The Nolan Frame: Composition and Symmetry..112

Chapter 7: Editing and Pacing: The Rhythm of a Nolan Film

Cross-Cutting and parallel action: Enhancing tension and drama. 115

Pacing for mystery and revelation.........................118

Time as a character: Manipulating pace to serve the narrative. 121

Scene analyses: Examining editing choices in "Memento" and "The Prestige." 124

Chapter 8: Soundtrack and Sound Design

The role of sound effects in Nolan's storytelling...127

The role of silence in Nolan's storytelling.............130

Collaboration with composers, especially Hans Zimmer: Themes and motifs. 133

Chapter 9: Legacy and Influence

Nolan's impact on independent and mainstream cinema...137

The future of filmmaking inspired by Nolan's techniques. 140

Appendix

Filmography of Christopher Nolan......................143

10 films to watch that inspired Nolan. 147

Glossary of film terms. 150

Chapter 1: Introduction to Christopher Nolan

Overview of Nolan's filmography.

Christopher Nolan's filmography is a testament to his prowess as a storyteller and a visionary director, whose work has significantly impacted modern cinema. His journey began with the 1998 feature, "Following," a noir thriller made on a shoestring budget that showcased Nolan's penchant for non-linear narratives and complex characters. This film set the tone for what would become hallmark traits of his career: innovative storytelling, deep psychological themes, and a unique visual style. Nolan's breakthrough came with "Memento" (2000), a psychological thriller that explores the themes of memory, identity, and perception through a reverse narrative structure. This film not only garnered critical acclaim but also established Nolan as a filmmaker capable of merging intricate plots with emotional depth.

The success of "Memento" paved the way for "Insomnia" (2002), a psychological thriller that allowed Nolan to work with high-profile actors like Al Pacino, Robin Williams, and Hilary Swank. Unlike his previous films, "Insomnia" adopted a more linear narrative but did not shy away from exploring complex characters and moral ambiguity. Nolan's exploration of the psychological depths of his characters continued with "The Prestige" (2006), a film about two rival magicians in late 19th century London. Here, Nolan delved into themes of obsession, sacrifice, and the consequences of relentless pursuit of greatness. Through these early films, Nolan demonstrated a unique ability to craft compelling narratives that challenge audiences' perceptions and engage them in deep, philosophical questions.

Christopher Nolan's name became synonymous with innovative blockbuster filmmaking with the release of "Batman Begins" (2005), which marked his foray into the superhero genre. Reimagining the Batman franchise, Nolan introduced a darker, more realistic portrayal of the character and his world, setting a new standard for superhero films. The sequel, "The Dark Knight" (2008), is widely regarded as one of the greatest films of the 21st century, praised for its complex characters, moral dilemmas, and Heath Ledger's iconic portrayal of the Joker. The film's success was not just commercial but also critical, proving that superhero films could be profound and thought-provoking. Nolan completed his Batman trilogy with "The Dark Knight Rises" (2012), a fitting conclusion that explored themes of redemption, legacy, and resilience. Together, these films not only revitalized the superhero genre but also cemented Nolan's status as a director capable of blending commercial appeal with artistic integrity.

Nolan's ambition and scope expanded further with "Inception" (2010) and "Interstellar" (2014), films that explored complex concepts like dreams within dreams and space-time travel. "Inception" is a masterclass in narrative complexity, visual effects, and emotional storytelling, while "Interstellar" combines human drama with theoretical physics, making profound statements about love, time, and humanity's place in the universe. Both films showcase Nolan's ability to create visually stunning, intellectually challenging, and emotionally engaging cinema that pushes the boundaries of the medium. His latest offerings, "Dunkirk" (2017) and "Tenet" (2020), further demonstrate his mastery in storytelling, with "Dunkirk" offering a visceral, immersive experience of the WWII evacuation and "Tenet" exploring time inversion in a spy thriller format. These films, characterized by their ambitious scale, intricate narratives, and groundbreaking use of practical effects and IMAX cameras, continue to challenge and expand the cinematic landscape.

Christopher Nolan's filmography is not just a collection of films but a milestone in cinematic history. His work transcends traditional genres, blending science fiction with psychological drama, fantasy with reality, and commercial blockbuster appeal with artistic depth. Nolan's films are distinguished by their thematic richness, exploring existential questions, the nature of reality, and the human condition. His use of non-linear storytelling, practical effects, and IMAX technology has revolutionized how stories are told on the big screen, making him one of the most influential filmmakers of our time. Through his visionary approach and unique narrative style, Nolan has created a body of work that continues to inspire and captivate audiences around the world, ensuring his place among the pantheon of great directors in cinema history.

Brief biography of early life.

Christopher Edward Nolan, born on July 30, 1970, in London, England, is a filmmaker whose early life significantly influenced his future in cinema. Nolan's dual British and American heritage, as a result of his English father and American mother, afforded him a bicultural upbringing that exposed him to a diverse range of perspectives from a young age. This unique background nurtured an early fascination with storytelling and film, laying the groundwork for his distinct narrative style that would later define his career. Growing up, Nolan split his time between London and Chicago, providing him with experiences that broadened his worldview and deepened his appreciation for cinematic storytelling across cultures. From an early age, Nolan was captivated by the magic of movies, a passion that was kindled by regular visits to the cinema with his family and the opportunity to explore the diverse cinematic landscapes of both Britain and America.

Nolan's journey into filmmaking began in earnest during his formative years. He started making short films with his father's Super 8 camera when he was just seven years old, demonstrating an early knack for storytelling and a keen interest in the mechanics of film production. These childhood experiments were Nolan's first forays into directing, editing, and cinematography, allowing him to develop his skills long before his professional career began. His early films, often starring action figures and involving elaborate plots, were a clear indication of his burgeoning talent and creativity. This period of exploration and experimentation was crucial in shaping Nolan's understanding of film as a medium for storytelling, an understanding that he would continue to refine throughout his career.

During his teenage years, Nolan's passion for film evolved into a serious pursuit of knowledge about cinema. He became an avid reader of film theory and history, absorbing the works of seminal filmmakers and critics. This self-guided education in the art and science of filmmaking deepened his appreciation for the craft and informed his developing aesthetic and thematic interests. Nolan's academic pursuits led him to University College London (UCL), where he chose to study English Literature—a decision that underscored his commitment to storytelling as the foundation of his filmmaking philosophy. At UCL, Nolan was actively involved in the university's film society, where he utilized the society's equipment and resources to produce a series of short films. This period was instrumental in honing his skills in writing, directing, and producing, providing him with valuable hands-on experience in film production.

Christopher Nolan's early life was a blend of cultural immersion, creative experimentation, and academic exploration, all of which played a pivotal role in his development as a filmmaker. His bicultural upbringing exposed him to a wide range of cinematic influences, nurturing a deep love for film that would become the cornerstone of his career. The hands-on experience gained from making short films in his youth equipped him with practical skills in filmmaking, while his academic background in literature enriched his storytelling abilities. These experiences, combined with his innate talent and passion for cinema, laid the foundation for Nolan's distinctive approach to filmmaking. As he transitioned from making short films to feature-length projects, Nolan carried with him the lessons learned during these formative years, setting the stage for a career that would redefine the possibilities of modern cinema.

His influences: From Kubrick to Bond.

Christopher Nolan's cinematic style is a rich tapestry woven from various influences, with Stanley Kubrick and the James Bond franchise standing out as significant touchstones in his development as a filmmaker. Kubrick's influence on Nolan is evident in numerous aspects of his work, from narrative complexity and thematic depth to visual aesthetics and the use of music. Kubrick, known for his meticulous attention to detail, mastery of film genre, and innovative techniques, left an indelible mark on Nolan, who has often spoken of his admiration for the legendary director. Nolan's interest in non-linear storytelling, as seen in "Memento," and his exploration of existential themes in films like "Inception" and "Interstellar," echo Kubrick's narrative ambition and philosophical inquiries in classics such as "2001: A Space Odyssey" and "The Shining." Moreover, Nolan's commitment to practical effects and in-camera techniques can be traced back to Kubrick's pioneering use of practical visual effects, further highlighting the profound impact Kubrick has had on Nolan's approach to filmmaking.

The James Bond series, with its blend of espionage, action, and spectacle, has also played a pivotal role in shaping Nolan's cinematic sensibilities. Nolan has openly expressed his fondness for the Bond films, citing them as a major influence on his work, particularly in the creation of the "Dark Knight" trilogy. The Bond franchise's integration of high-stakes drama, complex characters, and elaborate set pieces inspired Nolan to reimagine the superhero genre, infusing the Batman films with a sense of realism and psychological depth reminiscent of the best Bond films. The influence of the Bond series extends beyond the "Dark Knight" trilogy, as seen in "Inception," which Nolan has described as his own version of a Bond film. "Inception" incorporates elements typical of the Bond franchise, such as exotic locales, intricate action sequences, and a suave protagonist, while also embedding them within Nolan's trademark narrative and thematic complexity. This melding of influences showcases Nolan's ability to draw from his inspirations while pushing the boundaries of genre to create something wholly original.

In addition to Kubrick and Bond, Nolan's influences include a broad spectrum of filmmakers and genres, from the cerebral science fiction of Ridley Scott to the psychological thrillers of Alfred Hitchcock. Nolan's appreciation for Hitchcock's mastery of suspense and narrative tension is apparent in his own films, where he employs similar techniques to engage and manipulate the audience's emotions. Ridley Scott's "Blade Runner" has also been cited by Nolan as a key influence, particularly in its use of visual storytelling and world-building to convey complex themes and emotions. These diverse influences, combined with Nolan's unique vision and creativity, contribute to the distinctive style that has made his films critically acclaimed and commercially successful worldwide.

Christopher Nolan's filmography is a testament to the power of cinema as a medium for exploring complex ideas and pushing the envelope of narrative and visual storytelling. Through his integration of influences from Kubrick to Bond, along with a myriad of other sources, Nolan has crafted a body of work that is both intellectually stimulating and profoundly human. His films challenge audiences to think deeply about the nature of reality, time, and identity, while also providing the thrills and emotional engagement of mainstream cinema. As Nolan continues to evolve as a filmmaker, his influences serve as a foundation upon which he builds new worlds and stories, further cementing his status as one of the most innovative and influential directors of our time.

Early career and breakthrough with "Following" and "Memento."

Christopher Nolan's journey into the realms of professional filmmaking commenced with an audacious step through his debut feature, "Following," a project that encapsulated his nascent yet palpable storytelling prowess and set the stage for his subsequent breakthrough with "Memento." Nolan's early career was marked by a tenacious desire to craft compelling narratives within the constraints of limited resources. "Following," produced on a shoestring budget of just $6,000, was a striking demonstration of Nolan's inventive use of narrative structure and his ability to create a gripping cinematic experience from minimal resources. Filmed in black and white, "Following" tells the story of a young writer who starts following strangers around the streets of London, an obsession that draws him into the criminal underworld. The film's non-linear narrative, a hallmark of Nolan's later works, and its noir-inspired aesthetic showcased Nolan's early interest in themes of identity, voyeurism, and the blurred lines between observer and participant. Despite its limited budget and resources, "Following" garnered critical acclaim for its clever storytelling and visual style, earning a spot at various film festivals and capturing the attention of both audiences and critics. This initial success laid the groundwork for Nolan's next project, "Memento," which would catapult him into the spotlight as a filmmaker of unique vision and creativity.

"Memento," Nolan's sophomore feature, represented a significant breakthrough in his career, both in terms of narrative ambition and critical reception. Released in 2000, the film is a psychological thriller that employs a reverse chronological narrative to tell the story of Leonard Shelby, a man with anterograde amnesia who uses notes, tattoos, and Polaroid photos to hunt for his wife's killer. "Memento" was not only a showcase of Nolan's mastery over complex storytelling but also a profound exploration of memory, identity, and the subjective nature of truth. The film's innovative structure, which mirrored the protagonist's fragmented memory, challenged audiences to piece together the narrative, engaging them in an active process of discovery and interpretation. "Memento" received widespread acclaim for its originality, narrative depth, and Nolan's deft handling of the non-linear format, earning numerous awards and nominations, including Academy Award nominations for Best Original Screenplay and Best Film Editing. The film's success proved to be a turning point for Nolan, establishing him as a major talent in the industry and paving the way for his future projects. It demonstrated Nolan's ability to combine intellectual rigor with mainstream appeal, a balance that would define his subsequent work.

The early phase of Christopher Nolan's career, characterized by his work on "Following" and "Memento," reflects a filmmaker deeply committed to exploring the possibilities of narrative cinema. These films, though differing in scope and scale, share a common thread in their exploration of complex themes through innovative storytelling techniques. Nolan's approach to filmmaking during this period was marked by a willingness to take creative risks and push the boundaries of conventional narrative structures. His success with "Memento" in particular, highlighted his ability to engage both critics and audiences with a film that was intellectually challenging yet emotionally resonant. This balance between thought-provoking content and accessibility became a signature of Nolan's style and set the stage for his later, larger-scale projects. Through "Following" and "Memento," Nolan not only demonstrated his talent and vision as a filmmaker but also established a thematic and stylistic foundation that he would continue to build upon throughout his career. These early works underscore Nolan's dedication to the craft of filmmaking and his ability to transcend the limitations of budget and resources to create compelling, thought-provoking cinema.

Christopher Nolan's ascent from the independent success of "Following" to the groundbreaking triumph of "Memento" marks a significant period in his career, showcasing his evolution as a storyteller and his growing command over the medium of film. The critical and commercial success of "Memento" served as a springboard for Nolan, opening doors to larger and more ambitious projects. This early phase of his career not only solidified his reputation as a filmmaker capable of melding complex narratives with profound thematic depth but also demonstrated his unique ability to captivate audiences with his innovative approach to storytelling. Nolan's work on "Following" and "Memento" laid the groundwork for a career that would be defined by a continual pursuit of innovation, a commitment to exploring the human condition, and a relentless ambition to expand the boundaries of cinematic storytelling. Through these early films, Nolan established himself as a visionary director, whose career would continue to be marked by a dedication to pushing the limits of narrative structure, thematic exploration, and visual storytelling.

His place in modern cinema.

Christopher Nolan occupies a distinctive and influential position in modern cinema, blending complex narratives with blockbuster spectacle in a manner that has not only redefined genres but also elevated the expectations of audiences and critics alike. His films, characterized by innovative storytelling, technical prowess, and thematic depth, have garnered both critical acclaim and commercial success, making him one of the few directors to consistently bridge the gap between art-house sensibilities and mainstream appeal. Nolan's approach to filmmaking—marked by a preference for practical effects, reliance on film over digital, and the use of IMAX cameras—demonstrates a commitment to the cinematic experience that is increasingly rare in an era dominated by CGI and streaming platforms. This commitment has not only endeared him to cinephiles but has also set a benchmark for visual and narrative quality in Hollywood productions.

Moreover, Nolan's influence extends beyond the technical aspects of filmmaking; he has also made significant contributions to narrative structure and storytelling techniques. Films such as "Memento," "Inception," and "Interstellar" are notable for their non-linear narratives, complex themes, and existential questions, challenging audiences to engage with cinema in more intellectually active ways. By doing so, Nolan has played a pivotal role in making high-concept, thought-provoking content accessible to a wider audience, proving that blockbuster films can also be deeply meaningful and artistically ambitious. His work has inspired a new generation of filmmakers to explore innovative narrative techniques and thematic explorations within the constraints of mainstream cinema.

Nolan's filmography, which includes a successful reimagining of the superhero genre with "The Dark Knight" trilogy, has had a profound impact on how such stories are told. By infusing these films with a sense of realism, moral complexity, and psychological depth, Nolan elevated the superhero narrative, demonstrating that comic book movies could be serious works of art. This influence is evident in the subsequent wave of superhero films that have sought to emulate Nolan's blend of depth, darkness, and complexity. Moreover, his ability to craft engaging, original stories within the often formulaic confines of genre cinema has encouraged a more narrative-driven approach to blockbuster filmmaking, where character development and thematic richness are given as much priority as visual effects and action sequences.

Christopher Nolan's place in modern cinema is also marked by his advocacy for the theatrical experience. At a time when digital streaming services are becoming increasingly dominant, Nolan remains a staunch supporter of the traditional cinema-going experience, championing the importance of film as a communal, immersive event. His films are designed to be seen on the largest screens possible, with "Dunkirk" and "Tenet" serving as recent examples of his commitment to pushing the boundaries of visual and auditory immersion. Through his public statements and choices as a filmmaker, Nolan has become an important figure in the ongoing dialogue about the future of cinema, advocating for the preservation of film as a distinct artistic medium that deserves to be experienced in theaters.

Christopher Nolan's significant place in modern cinema can be attributed to his unique blend of narrative innovation, technical mastery, and a profound respect for the medium of film. His body of work not only challenges and delights audiences but also pushes the boundaries of what is possible in filmmaking, both from a storytelling and a technical perspective. Nolan has carved out a niche that straddles commercial success and artistic integrity, making him a pivotal figure in the contemporary cinematic landscape. His influence is felt not only in the content and structure of modern films but also in the broader discourse surrounding cinema, from the importance of the theatrical experience to the potential of films to provoke thought and engage audiences on a deeply intellectual level. As cinema continues to evolve, Nolan's contributions will undoubtedly remain a benchmark for filmmakers and a source of inspiration for audiences, securing his legacy as one of the most important and influential directors of his generation.

Chapter 2: Storytelling and Narrative Structure

His idea creation method.

Christopher Nolan's method of idea creation is a fascinating blend of personal interests, intellectual curiosity, and a deep engagement with complex themes, which together serve as the foundation for his unique storytelling approach. Nolan has often emphasized the importance of original ideas and the internal genesis of these ideas, which often stem from his contemplations and explorations of conceptual and philosophical questions. His films, known for their depth and complexity, begin as nascent thoughts that gradually evolve into intricate narratives. This process is reflective of Nolan's preference for developing his projects over extended periods, allowing ideas to mature and interconnect in innovative ways. For instance, the concept for "Inception" germinated in Nolan's mind for about a decade, during which he refined its intricate plot about dreams within dreams and the nature of reality. This slow cooking of ideas ensures that by the time Nolan is ready to pen a screenplay, the concept is fully developed, rich in detail, and ripe with thematic complexity.

Nolan's ideation process is also significantly influenced by his wide-ranging interests in science, philosophy, and psychology. He often integrates these disciplines into the fabric of his films, using them not only to advance the plot but also to deepen the audience's engagement with the narrative. "Interstellar," for example, was born out of Nolan's fascination with gravitational physics and the theories of time and space. This marriage of scientific curiosity with storytelling is a testament to Nolan's method of idea creation, where research and collaboration play key roles in transforming abstract concepts into compelling cinematic experiences.

Another hallmark of Nolan's approach to idea creation is his use of visual imagery as a tool for narrative development. Nolan is known for conceptualizing key images or scenes that serve as the emotional or visual centerpiece around which he constructs the rest of the film. This method is evident in the way he envisioned the rotating hallway fight sequence in "Inception" or the docking scene in "Interstellar" before the scripts were fully fleshed out. These images not only become iconic moments in the films but also act as narrative anchors, helping to guide the development of the plot and the characters' journeys. By starting with these vivid, imaginative concepts, Nolan ensures that his films are visually compelling and thematically integrated, with each visual choice reinforcing the narrative's underlying ideas.

Collaboration is yet another critical component of Nolan's idea creation process. While Nolan is the architect of his films' core concepts, he often refines and expands these ideas through collaborations with his trusted co-writers, producers, and technical advisors. His long-term partnership with his brother, Jonathan Nolan, has been particularly fruitful, with Jonathan contributing to the scripts of several of Nolan's most complex films, including "Memento" and "Interstellar." These collaborations allow Nolan to challenge and refine his ideas, ensuring that the final product is both intellectually rigorous and emotionally resonant. This method of idea creation, characterized by a blend of personal vision, interdisciplinary research, visual imagination, and collaborative refinement, underscores Nolan's role as a master storyteller, capable of weaving complex narratives that captivate and engage audiences around the world.

In essence, Christopher Nolan's method of creating ideas underscores a multifaceted approach that combines deep intellectual exploration with vivid visual storytelling and collaborative refinement. His films are distinguished not just by their narrative innovation and thematic depth but also by their capacity to provoke thought, stir emotions, and push the boundaries of conventional storytelling. Through his unique ideation process, Nolan continues to contribute to the evolution of cinema, crafting films that challenge audiences to think, question, and marvel. His work not only entertains but also enriches the cinematic landscape, leaving an indelible mark on the medium and its audiences.

Writing process and schedule.

Christopher Nolan's writing process is a testament to the discipline, creativity, and meticulous planning that characterizes his approach to filmmaking. For Nolan, writing is not merely a preliminary step in the creation of a film but a foundational phase that shapes the entire project. His writing schedule is marked by consistency and intensity, often involving long periods of isolation where he immerses himself in the world of the story he's crafting. This immersion is crucial, as Nolan believes in living within the narrative, exploring its possibilities, and understanding its characters deeply before translating the concept into a screenplay. He typically starts with extensive note-taking, jotting down ideas, research, and snippets of dialogue, which then gradually evolve into a structured outline. This phase can last for months or even years, as seen with "Inception," which Nolan pondered for a decade before finalizing the script. Such a prolonged gestation period allows Nolan to fully explore the thematic and narrative complexities of his ideas, ensuring that the script is both intellectually robust and emotionally compelling.

Once the foundational ideas are in place, Nolan transitions into a more intensive phase of the writing process, dedicating specific blocks of time each day to writing. He is known for his preference for writing in longhand, believing that the physical act of writing connects him more intimately with the story.

This methodical approach underscores the significance Nolan places on the screenplay, viewing it as the blueprint for the entire film. During this phase, Nolan works closely with his collaborators, particularly his brother Jonathan Nolan, with whom he has co-written several films. These collaborations allow for a dynamic exchange of ideas, refining and enriching the script through dialogue and feedback. Nolan's writing process is thus both solitary and collaborative, allowing him to maintain a clear vision for the film while also being open to new perspectives and insights.

The final stages of Nolan's writing process involve meticulous revision, where every element of the script is scrutinized and polished. Nolan pays close attention to the structure, pacing, and dialogue, ensuring that the narrative flows seamlessly and that the characters' voices are distinct and authentic. He also integrates his technical knowledge into the writing process, considering how the script's visual and auditory elements will be realized on screen. This holistic approach to writing, where narrative, character, and cinematic techniques are interwoven from the outset, is key to the coherence and impact of Nolan's films. It reflects his belief that a film's power lies not just in its story or themes but in how these elements are executed through the medium of cinema.

Christopher Nolan's writing process and schedule highlight his dedication to the craft of filmmaking.

Through disciplined planning, creative exploration, and meticulous revision, Nolan crafts narratives that are not only complex and thought-provoking but also emotionally resonant and visually spectacular. His approach to writing emphasizes the importance of the screenplay in shaping the cinematic experience, demonstrating that at the heart of every great film is a powerful story, meticulously told. This commitment to storytelling, combined with his innovative vision and technical mastery, has established Nolan as one of the most influential filmmakers of his generation, whose work continues to push the boundaries of what cinema can achieve.

Analysis of the art of misdirection: Plot twists and reveals in "The Prestige" and "Inception."

Christopher Nolan's mastery of the art of misdirection is exemplified in his films "The Prestige" (2006) and "Inception" (2010), where he utilizes plot twists and reveals not merely as narrative devices, but as integral elements that deepen the thematic exploration and emotional impact of the stories. In "The Prestige," Nolan crafts a tale of obsession, sacrifice, and the dark consequences of rivalry between two magicians in Victorian London. The film is structured around the three acts of a magic trick: the pledge, the turn, and the prestige, which Nolan ingeniously applies to the film's narrative structure itself. Throughout the film, Nolan employs misdirection, leading the audience to focus on the bitter rivalry and the lengths to which each magician will go to outdo the other. However, the true reveal, or "prestige," of the film lies in the personal sacrifices they make and the obsession that consumes them. The twist ending not only surprises but also reframes the entire narrative, prompting viewers to reconsider the moral complexities and personal costs of the characters' pursuits. This narrative sleight of hand mirrors the themes of illusion and sacrifice, engaging the audience in a deeper reflection on the nature of obsession and the price of ambition.

"Inception," on the other hand, delves into the world of dreams within dreams, creating a complex narrative labyrinth that blurs the lines between reality and illusion. Nolan uses the concept of inception – planting an idea in someone's mind through a dream – as a foundation for exploring themes of guilt, redemption, and the power of the subconscious. The film's structure, with its layers of dreams, serves as a form of misdirection, focusing the audience's attention on the heist-style plot and the technical intricacies of navigating the dream world. However, the emotional core of the film lies in Cobb's (Leonardo DiCaprio) personal journey to confront his guilt and make peace with his past. The final scene, with the ambiguous fate of the spinning top, serves as the ultimate misdirection, leaving the audience questioning the nature of reality. This open-ended conclusion is not merely a narrative twist but a thematic reflection on the film's exploration of dreams, memory, and the subjective nature of reality. Nolan's use of misdirection in "Inception" invites the audience to engage with the film on multiple levels, pondering not only the technicalities of the plot but also the deeper emotional and existential questions it raises.

The art of misdirection in "The Prestige" and "Inception" is a testament to Nolan's skill as a storyteller, capable of weaving complex narratives that captivate and intrigue while also engaging with profound themes. In both films, Nolan demonstrates an understanding of misdirection not just as a plot device, but as a means to enrich the narrative and invite deeper contemplation. By carefully constructing twists and reveals, he challenges the audience's perceptions and expectations, leading them on a journey that is as intellectually stimulating as it is emotionally resonant. This approach not only showcases Nolan's narrative dexterity but also his ability to engage audiences in a dialogue that extends beyond the confines of the screen. The twists and turns of the plot become a vehicle for exploring larger human experiences and dilemmas, making the films enduring works of cinema that invite repeated viewing and sustained reflection.

Christopher Nolan's use of plot twists and reveals in "The Prestige" and "Inception" highlights his masterful use of misdirection to deepen thematic exploration and enhance narrative complexity.

Through these films, Nolan not only entertains but also provokes thought, exploring the boundaries between reality and illusion, the depths of human obsession, and the intricacies of the subconscious. His ability to surprise and challenge audiences, while also engaging them in profound thematic discussions, cements his status as a filmmaker who transcends conventional storytelling. The art of misdirection, in Nolan's hands, becomes an essential tool in crafting narratives that are both intellectually rewarding and emotionally compelling, solidifying his place in the pantheon of great contemporary filmmakers.

Analysis of non-linear storytelling in "Memento, " "Inception," and "Dunkirk."

Christopher Nolan's foray into non-linear storytelling is not merely a stylistic choice but a profound narrative strategy that significantly enhances the thematic depth and emotional engagement of his films. "Memento" (2000), "Inception" (2010), and "Dunkirk" (2017) each utilize non-linear narrative techniques to varying degrees and purposes, showcasing Nolan's versatility and ingenuity as a storyteller. In "Memento," Nolan employs a reverse chronological order to immerse the audience into the fragmented and unreliable perspective of the protagonist, Leonard Shelby, who suffers from short-term memory loss. This narrative choice is not just a clever plot device; it serves as a direct representation of Leonard's condition, forcing the audience to piece together the story as Leonard does, moment by moment. The structure of "Memento" challenges conventional narrative and viewer expectation, requiring active engagement as the plot unfolds in reverse, revealing key information in a manner that continually reshapes the audience's understanding of the characters and their motivations. This method of storytelling effectively simulates Leonard's experience of memory loss and disorientation, deepening the audience's empathy for his plight and engagement with the narrative's exploration of memory, identity, and truth.

"Inception" takes the concept of non-linear storytelling and layers it within the multi-leveled dream sequences that form the crux of the film's plot. Here, Nolan constructs a narrative that operates across several tiers of reality simultaneously, with each level of the dream having its own flow of time. The complexity of "Inception's" structure is a technical marvel, serving not just to dazzle but to encapsulate the film's exploration of the subconscious, the nature of ideas, and the blurring of lines between reality and illusion. As the narrative weaves through these various layers, the audience is compelled to navigate the labyrinthine plot alongside the characters, piecing together a puzzle that spans the deeply personal to the universally existential. This intricate structure reinforces the themes of inception and manipulation, mirroring the process of idea formation and the impact of the subconscious on perceived reality. The non-linear storytelling of "Inception" not only drives the narrative forward but also embeds within it a deeper meditation on the power of the mind, the fragility of reality, and the complexity of human emotion.

"Dunkirk" represents another innovative approach to non-linear storytelling, with Nolan choosing to depict the historic evacuation from three different perspectives – land, sea, and air – each with its own distinct timeline. The narratives converge and diverge over the course of the film, creating a tapestry of experiences that captures the chaos, uncertainty, and desperation of the Dunkirk evacuation. Unlike "Memento" and "Inception," where the non-linear narrative serves to delve into the psychological and existential, "Dunkirk" uses it to evoke a visceral sense of time and place, amplifying the intensity and immediacy of the historical event. This approach allows Nolan to explore the themes of time, survival, and the collective effort in the face of adversity, presenting the evacuation as a mosaic of human experiences rather than a singular, unified narrative. The temporal disjunctions serve to heighten the suspense and highlight the synchronicity of actions and decisions across different theaters of war, emphasizing the interconnectedness of individual and collective fates.

Through "Memento," "Inception," and "Dunkirk," Christopher Nolan has not only demonstrated the versatility of non-linear storytelling but also its potential to deepen narrative complexity and thematic richness. Each film employs this technique to different ends, whether exploring the intricacies of memory and identity, the layers of reality and dreams, or the collective experience of historical trauma. Nolan's innovative use of non-linear narrative structures challenges traditional storytelling conventions and audience expectations, demanding active engagement and offering rich, multifaceted explorations of complex themes. This approach not only distinguishes Nolan as a filmmaker but also enriches the cinematic experience, inviting viewers to engage with his films on multiple levels – intellectually, emotionally, and philosophically.

Creating believable worlds: "Inception" and "Interstellar."

In the realm of contemporary cinema, Christopher Nolan stands out for his exceptional ability to create immersive, believable worlds that captivate audiences and provoke deep thought. His films "Inception" (2010) and "Interstellar" (2014) are prime examples of this talent, showcasing his aptitude not only for storytelling but also for constructing detailed, plausible universes that serve as the foundation for his narratives. "Inception" explores the intricate world of dreams within dreams, where the human subconscious becomes the battleground for corporate espionage. Nolan meticulously crafts this universe with a set of rules that govern dream manipulation, extraction, and inception, delving into the architecture of the mind with a level of detail that lends the film a tangible sense of reality. The concept of a "dream within a dream" is explored through a well-defined framework that includes the time dilation experienced at different levels of the subconscious, the importance of dream "architecture," and the psychological implications of diving too deep into the human psyche. This attention to detail, combined with the film's innovative visual effects and narrative complexity, creates a world that is both fantastical and eerily plausible. Nolan's success in "Inception" lies in his ability to ground the film's more fantastical elements in the human experience, using the dream world to explore themes of grief, guilt, and the quest for redemption.

"Interstellar" takes Nolan's world-building prowess to the cosmic scale, blending theoretical physics with a deeply human story of love, sacrifice, and survival. Set in a near-future where Earth is on the brink of collapse, "Interstellar" explores the vastness of space through the lens of a desperate mission to find humanity a new home. Nolan, working closely with physicist Kip Thorne, ensures that the film's depiction of space travel, black holes, and time dilation is rooted in current scientific understanding, lending the film an air of authenticity despite its speculative premise. The visual representation of these phenomena, such as the rendering of the black hole Gargantua, is not only stunning but also scientifically informed, making "Interstellar" a landmark in the portrayal of space in cinema. Beyond the scientific accuracy, the film excels in creating a believable world through its depiction of human resilience and the emotional ties that bind us, even across galaxies. The relationship between the protagonist, Cooper, and his daughter, Murph, serves as the emotional core of the film, grounding the interstellar journey in a relatable human story. This balance between the scientific and the emotional, the cosmic and the intimate, makes "Interstellar" a compelling exploration of humanity's place in the universe.

Creating believable worlds in "Inception" and "Interstellar" goes beyond the mere technicalities of dream layers and space travel; it involves weaving complex human emotions and relationships into the fabric of these universes. Nolan's worlds are inhabited by characters who face not only the external challenges of their environments but also internal conflicts and moral dilemmas that resonate with the audience. In "Inception," the dream world is as much a place of wonder and possibility as it is a prison for Cobb, the protagonist, who is haunted by his memories and guilt. Similarly, in "Interstellar," the vastness of space and the scientific quest for a new home are juxtaposed with the personal sacrifices made by the astronauts and the families they leave behind. This interplay between the vast, impersonal scope of the universe and the intimate, personal scale of human experience is what makes Nolan's worlds so believable and immersive. By grounding his narratives in universal human emotions while painstakingly constructing the rules and details of his universes, Nolan invites the audience to suspend disbelief and embark on a journey that is as intellectually stimulating as it is emotionally engaging.

"Inception" and "Interstellar" exemplify Christopher Nolan's exceptional skill in creating believable worlds that serve as the backdrop for exploring complex themes and human experiences. Through meticulous attention to detail, scientific accuracy, and a deep understanding of the human condition, Nolan crafts narratives that are not only visually stunning and conceptually ambitious but also emotionally resonant. His ability to balance the grandeur and complexity of the worlds he creates with the intricacies of human emotion and relationships ensures that these films transcend their speculative genres, offering audiences a deeply immersive and thought-provoking experience. Nolan's worlds are not just settings for his stories; they are integral to them, shaping and reflecting the journeys of their characters. In doing so, Nolan not only pushes the boundaries of cinematic world-building but also enriches the medium's capacity for storytelling.

The rule of realism: Grounding the extraordinary

Christopher Nolan's filmmaking is distinguished by his commitment to grounding the extraordinary in realism, a rule that has become a signature across his body of work. This approach not only enhances the believability of his narrative universes but also deepens the audience's emotional engagement with the story. Nolan's dedication to realism, especially in films dealing with fantastical or high-concept premises, is achieved through meticulous research, the use of practical effects, and the integration of real-world physics and philosophy into his storytelling. This blend of the real and the fantastic allows Nolan to explore complex themes and ideas while maintaining a sense of authenticity and relatability.

In "Inception," a film that delves into the intricacies of the human subconscious through dream invasion, Nolan grounds the science fiction premise in a meticulously crafted rule-based system. The dreams within dreams concept, while fantastical, is presented with such detailed rules and logic that it invites the audience to suspend disbelief. Nolan's use of practical effects, such as the rotating hallway fight scene, further cements the film's commitment to realism, offering a physicality to the dream sequences that CGI alone could not achieve. The integration of psychological and philosophical concepts related to memory, grief, and the nature of reality lends "Inception" a depth that resonates on a human level, making the extraordinary elements of the narrative feel plausible and impactful.

Nolan's rule of realism extends beyond the use of practical effects and scientific accuracy; it permeates his narrative choices and character development. His characters are complex, flawed individuals who face moral dilemmas and emotional turmoil, grounding even the most extraordinary stories in the universal human experience. This approach is evident in "The Dark Knight" trilogy, where Nolan reimagines the superhero genre through a lens of moral complexity and realism. Gotham City is portrayed not as a comic book caricature but as a living, breathing city with political, social, and economic challenges that mirror those of real-world urban centers. The trilogy's exploration of themes such as justice, chaos, and heroism is anchored in a nuanced understanding of human nature and society, lending a sense of authenticity and relevance to the fantastical elements of the Batman mythos.

By adhering to the rule of realism, Christopher Nolan accomplishes a delicate balancing act, weaving together the extraordinary and the believable in a manner that captivates and resonates with audiences. This commitment to grounding his films in reality, whether through technical means or narrative depth, allows Nolan to explore grand ideas and speculative worlds while maintaining a connection to the human condition. It is this blend of the fantastical with the real that defines Nolan's cinematic vision, making his films not only visually stunning and conceptually ambitious but also deeply human and emotionally compelling. Nolan's approach demonstrates that even the most extraordinary stories can be made relatable and impactful through a commitment to realism, offering audiences a richer, more immersive cinematic experience.

Chapter 3: The Psychological Depth: Characters and Themes

The recurring themes and motifs across his films.

Christopher Nolan's filmography is distinguished by its exploration of complex themes and motifs, which recur across his body of work, creating a cohesive narrative fabric that weaves through his diverse array of films. Among these, the manipulation of time stands out as a central preoccupation. Nolan's fascination with time's fluidity and its impact on human consciousness and perception is evident in films like "Memento," where the narrative unfolds in reverse chronological order to mimic the protagonist's memory loss, and "Inception," which plays with the concept of time dilation within dreams. In "Interstellar," time becomes a physical dimension that the characters navigate, highlighting its relativity and the profound implications it has on their lives and relationships. This thematic exploration goes beyond mere narrative technique; it delves into the philosophical implications of time, memory, and their role in shaping identity and reality. By repeatedly tackling the concept of time, Nolan invites viewers to contemplate its influence on their understanding of the past, the present, and the future, making time a character in its own right within his cinematic universe.

Another recurring theme in Nolan's work is the exploration of identity and the self. His films often feature protagonists on a quest for truth, not just about the world around them but also about their own nature. In "Memento," Leonard seeks to solve a mystery using an external system of notes and tattoos as a substitute for his memory, raising questions about the reliability of memory and its role in defining who we are. "The Dark Knight" trilogy examines Bruce Wayne's dual identity as Batman and his struggle to reconcile these two halves of himself. "Inception" further complicates this theme by introducing the idea of dreams as spaces where characters can lose themselves or discover deeper truths about their desires and guilt. Through these narratives, Nolan explores the fluidity of identity, the masks people wear, and the often-blurred line between reality and illusion, prompting audiences to reflect on their perceptions of self and the constructs that define individuality.

Moral ambiguity and the consequences of one's actions are also central to Nolan's cinematic discourse. His characters frequently inhabit morally complex worlds where right and wrong are not easily discernible. "The Dark Knight" presents a Gotham City rife with corruption and moral decay, forcing Batman to confront the ethical implications of his vigilantism. In "Inception," Cobb's mission to implant an idea in another's mind raises questions about the morality of influencing another person's subconscious. "Interstellar" and "Dunkirk" showcase characters making life-and-death decisions under extreme circumstances, highlighting the weight of responsibility and the ethical dilemmas inherent in survival and sacrifice. Through these stories, Nolan examines the nature of morality in a nuanced manner, challenging viewers to consider the gray areas in ethical decision-making and the ripple effects of their choices.

Finally, Nolan's films often grapple with the theme of existential angst and the search for meaning in an uncertain world. Characters across his oeuvre are confronted with existential crises that force them to question the nature of their reality, their purpose, and their place in the universe. In "Interstellar," humanity faces extinction, prompting a reflection on the significance of human endeavor and the legacy we leave behind. "Inception" explores the construction of reality and the power of ideas, while "The Prestige" delves into the destructive nature of obsession and the cost of pursuing greatness. Through these narratives, Nolan probes deep philosophical questions, inviting his audience to ponder their own existence and the human condition. This existential inquiry, coupled with his exploration of time, identity, and morality, forms the thematic core of Nolan's work, making his films not only visually and narratively compelling but also richly philosophical and introspective.

In weaving these themes and motifs throughout his films, Christopher Nolan has crafted a distinctive narrative landscape that challenges and engages audiences. His exploration of time, identity, moral ambiguity, and existential angst reflects a deep interest in the human experience, making his body of work a profound contribution to contemporary cinema. Through his innovative storytelling and thematic depth, Nolan invites viewers on a journey that is as intellectually stimulating as it is emotionally resonant, securing his place as one of the most visionary filmmakers of his generation.

Identity and memory: Dissecting "Memento" and "The Prestige."

Christopher Nolan's exploration of identity and memory is perhaps most intricately portrayed in his films "Memento" (2000) and "The Prestige" (2006). These films delve deep into the human psyche, presenting complex narratives that challenge conventional perceptions of self and the reliability of memory. In "Memento," Nolan constructs a reverse chronological narrative that mirrors the protagonist Leonard's anterograde amnesia—his inability to form new memories. This narrative structure immerses the audience in Leonard's fragmented reality, where memory, or the lack thereof, becomes a prison from which he cannot escape. Leonard's quest to find his wife's killer and his reliance on photographs, notes, and tattoos as substitutes for memory raise profound questions about identity. Without memory as a foundation,

Leonard's sense of self is unstable and easily manipulated by those around him. Nolan uses Leonard's condition to explore the idea that our memories, however flawed, form the bedrock of our identity. They shape our perceptions, decisions, and relationships. The film suggests that without memory, one's sense of self becomes a narrative constructed from external sources, vulnerable to alteration and deception. "Memento" not only dissects the relationship between identity and memory but also comments on the human need for closure and the lengths to which people will go to achieve it, regardless of the truth.

"The Prestige," on the other hand, presents a different but equally complex exploration of identity, this time within the context of obsession and sacrifice. The film revolves around two rival magicians, Robert Angier and Alfred Borden, whose competition drives them to extremes in the pursuit of the perfect illusion. Nolan uses the backdrop of magic and illusion to delve into the themes of identity and duality. Borden's secret, which is central to the film's twist, exemplifies the split between personal identity and public persona, as well as the cost of living a life built on deception. The lengths to which both magicians go to conceal their secrets and surpass each other blur the lines between their true selves and the characters they portray on stage and in life. "The Prestige" interrogates the nature of identity when it is contingent upon the perception of others and the obsession with legacy. It also examines the role of memory in shaping one's identity, as both Angier and Borden are driven by past events that have left deep emotional scars. Their memories fuel their obsession, demonstrating how past experiences can define or distort one's sense of self. Nolan weaves a narrative that questions whether true identity can be known or if it is as malleable and susceptible to illusion as any magic trick.

Both "Memento" and "The Prestige" utilize non-linear storytelling to heighten the impact of their themes. In "Memento," the reverse chronological order disorients the viewer, replicating Leonard's experience of memory loss and forcing the audience to question the reliability of what they see and hear. This narrative choice emphasizes the film's exploration of identity and memory, as the audience must piece together Leonard's story and identity from fragmented snippets, much like Leonard himself. In "The Prestige," the narrative is interspersed with diary entries and flashbacks, creating a layered story that reveals the characters' secrets and true selves gradually. This structure mirrors the film's thematic focus on the illusions people create and the hidden truths that define their identities. Nolan's use of these storytelling techniques serves to engage the audience actively in the unraveling of the narrative, making the themes of identity and memory more resonant and thought-provoking.

Christopher Nolan's "Memento" and "The Prestige" are masterful examinations of the complex relationship between identity and memory. Through innovative narrative structures and compelling character studies, Nolan explores how our sense of self is constructed and the role memory plays in that process. He delves into the darkness of obsession and the lengths to which individuals will go to preserve their identity or create a new one. Both films challenge viewers to consider the stability of their own identities and the memories that shape them. Nolan's exploration is a testament to his skill as a filmmaker, capable of weaving complex philosophical inquiries into engaging narratives. These films underscore the idea that identity is not a fixed state but a fluid construct, shaped by our memories, perceptions, and the narratives we tell ourselves and others. Through "Memento" and "The Prestige," Nolan invites audiences into a deep reflection on the nature of self, memory, and the illusions that pervade both.

Morality and redemption: Character arcs in "The Dark Knight Trilogy."

Christopher Nolan's "The Dark Knight Trilogy" is a profound exploration of morality and redemption, themes that are woven through the character arcs of its protagonists and antagonists alike. Throughout "Batman Begins" (2005), "The Dark Knight" (2008), and "The Dark Knight Rises" (2012), Nolan redefines the superhero genre, presenting a gritty, realistic portrayal of Gotham City and its inhabitants. The trilogy's central character, Bruce Wayne/Batman, portrayed by Christian Bale, is a study in the complexity of moral decision-making and the quest for redemption. In "Batman Begins," Wayne's journey is initiated by personal loss and fueled by a desire for justice. His transformation into Batman is driven by a moral imperative to rid Gotham of the crime and corruption that claimed his parents' lives. However, Wayne's vigilante justice is fraught with ethical dilemmas, notably the fine line between justice and vengeance, and the responsibility that comes with power. Nolan carefully constructs Wayne's character arc to question the morality of Batman's actions and the sacrifices required for redemption. Wayne's struggle is not only against the external forces threatening Gotham but also an internal battle to reconcile his dual identity and the implications of his choices on his soul and the city he vows to protect.

"The Dark Knight" delves deeper into the theme of morality through the introduction of the Joker, a character who embodies chaos and seeks to disrupt the moral order of Gotham. The Joker's anarchic philosophy forces Batman, and by extension Gotham's citizens, to confront their moral limits and the darkness within themselves. Nolan uses the Joker as a catalyst to explore the theme of redemption, particularly through the character arc of Harvey Dent/Two-Face. Dent's tragic fall from Gotham's

"White Knight" to a vengeful murderer represents the fragility of morality and the ease with which hope can be corrupted. Batman's decision to take the blame for Dent's crimes at the end of "The Dark Knight" is a pivotal moment in the trilogy, underscoring the complexity of redemption. Batman sacrifices his reputation for the greater good, embodying the idea that true redemption often requires personal sacrifice and the willingness to bear the weight of difficult moral choices. This act sets the stage for the final chapter in the trilogy, where the consequences of Batman's sacrifice and the themes of morality and redemption reach their culmination.

In "The Dark Knight Rises," Nolan brings Bruce Wayne's journey full circle, challenging him to rise once more in the face of despair and defeat. The film examines the cost of redemption, both physically and emotionally, as Wayne confronts his own limitations and the legacy of his actions as Batman. The introduction of Bane as the antagonist, who seeks to complete Ra's al Ghul's mission to destroy Gotham, serves as a stark reminder of the unintended consequences of Wayne's earlier decisions. Wayne's struggle to reclaim his identity as Batman and save Gotham is not just a battle for the city's soul but also his own. His eventual success in defeating Bane and passing the mantle of Batman to John Blake suggests that redemption is possible, but it requires acceptance of the past and the courage to move forward. Wayne's ability to find peace and a new life beyond Batman symbolizes the ultimate redemption, both for himself and for Gotham. The trilogy concludes with a powerful message about the enduring nature of hope and the possibility of redemption, even in the darkest of times.

"The Dark Knight Trilogy" stands as a testament to Christopher Nolan's ability to weave complex themes of morality and redemption into the fabric of a superhero narrative. Through the character arcs of Bruce Wayne, Harvey Dent, and the city of Gotham itself, Nolan explores the nuanced nature of justice, the cost of vengeance, and the path to redemption. The trilogy challenges audiences to reflect on their own moral compasses and the sacrifices required for redemption. Nolan's masterful storytelling, combined with compelling character development and a realistic portrayal of the struggle between good and evil, elevates "The Dark Knight Trilogy" beyond a mere series of superhero films to a profound meditation on the human condition.

Obsession and sacrifice: The human element in "Interstellar" and "Inception."

Christopher Nolan's films often navigate the complexities of human emotion against a backdrop of high-concept, visually spectacular settings. "Interstellar" (2014) and "Inception" (2010) are prime examples, where the themes of obsession and sacrifice are explored in depth, providing a rich tapestry of the human element within these narratives. In "Interstellar," the Earth is on the brink of becoming uninhabitable, prompting a desperate mission to find humanity a new home among the stars. The film's protagonist, Cooper, portrayed by Matthew McConaughey, embodies the theme of sacrifice through his decision to leave his family behind, possibly forever, to pilot the mission. This choice is driven by an obsession not only with saving humanity but also with ensuring a future for his children. Nolan meticulously crafts this narrative to highlight the personal sacrifices made in the pursuit of a greater good. Cooper's journey through wormholes and across galaxies is underscored by his relentless desire to return to his family, a poignant reminder of the personal costs of his mission. The film intertwines the vast, impersonal expanse of space with the intimate, deeply human desire to protect and provide for one's loved ones, illustrating the sacrifices inherent in the quest for survival and exploration.

"Inception," on the other hand, delves into the world of corporate espionage through the manipulation of dreams, where Dom Cobb, played by Leonardo DiCaprio, is obsessed with the idea of returning home to his children. His journey into the layers of the subconscious is not only a professional endeavor but also a deeply personal quest for redemption. Cobb's sacrifice is evident in his willingness to navigate the treacherous landscape of the mind, risking his sanity, to plant an idea that will free him from his past. This obsession with achieving the impossible reflects the film's broader exploration of the sacrifices individuals make for personal liberation and reconciliation with their pasts. Nolan uses the dreamscapes of "Inception" to create a metaphor for the inner workings of the human psyche, revealing the depths of obsession and the high stakes of personal sacrifice. The film's climax, which leaves Cobb's reality ambiguous, serves as a profound commentary on the nature of sacrifice and obsession, suggesting that the line between reality and illusion can blur when one is deeply consumed by a singular goal.

Both "Interstellar" and "Inception" are characterized by Nolan's ability to blend groundbreaking cinematic techniques with deeply human stories of obsession and sacrifice. These themes are not merely narrative devices but are central to understanding the characters' motivations and the lengths to which they will go to achieve their goals. In "Interstellar," the theme of sacrifice extends beyond Cooper's personal story to encompass the entire crew of the Endurance, each member of which has left behind their old lives in pursuit of a new future for humanity. Their journey highlights the collective human capacity for sacrifice, underscoring the film's optimistic view of human resilience and cooperation. "Inception," meanwhile, presents a more introspective look at obsession, with Cobb's personal mission revealing how fixation on a single goal can consume and distort one's reality. Through these films, Nolan posits that obsession and sacrifice are two sides of the same coin, each driving individuals to extremes in pursuit of their objectives, whether they be the salvation of humanity or the reunification with loved ones.

In exploring these themes, Christopher Nolan reveals the fundamental human struggle to balance personal desires with the broader implications of our actions. "Interstellar" and "Inception" showcase the director's fascination with the human condition, set against the backdrop of complex, otherworldly phenomena. Through the stories of Cooper and Cobb, Nolan probes the depths of human emotion, from the anguish of separation to the relentless pursuit of a seemingly unattainable goal. These narratives are a testament to Nolan's skill in weaving the universal themes of obsession and sacrifice into the fabric of speculative, high-concept stories, highlighting the indomitable human spirit. In doing so, Nolan not only crafts visually stunning cinematic experiences but also poignant reflections on the essence of humanity, making "Interstellar" and "Inception" enduring works that resonate with audiences on a deeply emotional level.

Complex villains: The Joker, Bane, and beyond.

Christopher Nolan has redefined the portrayal of villains in cinema, particularly with the characters of

The Joker in "The Dark Knight" (2008) and Bane in "The Dark Knight Rises" (2012). These antagonists stand out not only for their formidable presence and direct challenge to Batman but also for their complex motivations and philosophical underpinnings. The Joker, portrayed by Heath Ledger in an Oscar-winning performance, is an agent of chaos who seeks to undermine Gotham's social order and reveal the fragility of morality. Unlike typical villains motivated by greed or personal vendetta, The Joker's motivations are philosophical, aiming to demonstrate that anyone can be corrupted under the right circumstances. His anarchistic view of the world challenges not just Batman but the audience's understanding of morality and justice. The Joker's complexity lies in his lack of a traditional backstory or clear motivations, making him an unpredictable force of nature. His belief that chaos is the natural order of the world puts him in direct opposition to Batman's quest for justice, setting the stage for a battle that is as much ideological as it is physical. The Joker's character raises questions about the nature of evil and the limits of heroism, making him one of the most memorable and discussed villains in modern cinema.

Bane, introduced in "The Dark Knight Rises," offers a different but equally complex challenge to Batman and Gotham. Portrayed by Tom Hardy, Bane is a physical and intellectual force, imposing a revolutionary ideology that seeks to dismantle

Gotham's existing power structures under the guise of liberating its citizens. Unlike The Joker, Bane's motivations are rooted in a distorted desire for equity, driven by his own experiences of injustice and suffering. His strength and strategy make him a formidable opponent, but it is his conviction and charismatic leadership that pose the greatest threat, as he convinces many to join his cause. Bane's complexity as a villain comes from his ability to exploit genuine societal grievances for his anarchistic ends, blurring the lines between villainy and vigilantism. His character examines themes of power, revolution, and the cyclical nature of oppression, adding depth to the narrative conflict and challenging Batman's role as a symbol of hope and order.

Nolan's villains extend beyond The Joker and Bane, each embodying a philosophical challenge to the protagonist and reflecting broader thematic concerns. In "Inception," for instance, the antagonist is not a person but rather the idea of doubt within Cobb's own mind. This internal struggle is as compelling as any physical villain, representing the human capacity for self-sabotage and the power of guilt and grief. Similarly, in "Interstellar," Dr. Mann, played by Matt Damon, embodies the darker aspects of human nature—self-preservation and cowardice—posing existential questions about mankind's readiness to transcend its limitations. Nolan's approach to crafting villains goes beyond mere character development; it involves integrating them into the fabric of the narrative in a way that they become essential to the exploration of the film's central themes. This method results in antagonists who are not only memorable for their deeds but also for their contribution to the narrative's philosophical depth.

Christopher Nolan's creation of complex villains like The Joker and Bane highlights his nuanced approach to character development and his interest in exploring moral and existential dilemmas through the lens of blockbuster cinema. These characters are not evil for the sake of being antagonists; they are deeply integrated into the thematic fabric of their respective films, challenging both the protagonists and the audience to reconsider their views on morality, justice, and the human condition. Nolan's villains stand out because they offer a mirror to society's flaws and fears, making them not only formidable foes for the heroes but also compelling figures for the audience to analyze and understand. Through these characters, Nolan elevates the superhero genre, turning comic book villains into complex characters that resonate on a deeply human level.

The antagonist's purpose: Driving the narrative forward.

In Christopher Nolan's filmography, antagonists play a pivotal role beyond merely opposing the protagonist; they drive the narrative forward, challenge the thematic exploration, and often serve as the catalyst for character development and plot progression. Nolan's antagonists are not merely obstacles but integral elements that add depth and complexity to the story, pushing protagonists to their limits and forcing them to confront their flaws, fears, and moral convictions. This dynamic is vividly illustrated in "The Dark Knight" (2008), where The Joker's anarchistic philosophy and actions precipitate a crisis in Gotham that tests the resolve and ethics of both Batman and the city's institutions. The Joker's purpose transcends his criminal undertakings, as he seeks to demonstrate the fragility of society's moral fabric and the ease with which it can be unraveled. Through his orchestrated chaos, The Joker challenges Batman's ideology, forcing the hero to confront the implications and sustainability of his vigilantism. This antagonistic force propels the narrative by deepening the thematic discourse on justice, order, and chaos, and by compelling Batman to evolve in response to these challenges. The Joker's presence and actions are fundamental in driving the story's progression, shaping its moral quandaries, and ultimately, facilitating a deeper understanding of the protagonist's character.

In "Inception" (2010), Nolan crafts a different kind of antagonist in the form of Mal, Cobb's deceased wife who exists as a projection in the dream world. Mal's appearances serve as a haunting reminder of Cobb's guilt and unresolved grief, embodying the internal conflict that he must overcome to achieve his goal. Unlike traditional antagonists, Mal does not have an agenda against the world but represents the protagonist's personal demons that hinder his journey. Her purpose is deeply intertwined with the film's exploration of memory, guilt, and redemption. By confronting the manifestation of Mal in his subconscious, Cobb is forced to face his past and the mistakes that have shaped him. This confrontation is crucial for both Cobb's emotional arc and the narrative's progression, as it adds layers to the complexity of the task at hand and elevates the stakes of the heist. Mal's role as an antagonist is subtle yet profound, driving the narrative by compelling Cobb to reconcile with his inner turmoil, thereby ensuring the mission's success and his personal redemption.

Furthermore, "Interstellar" (2014) introduces Dr. Mann as a compelling antagonist whose actions significantly drive the narrative forward. Mann, once revered as the best among the astronauts, embodies the darker aspects of human nature—desperation, cowardice, and the instinct for survival at any cost. His betrayal is a turning point in the film, adding tension and urgency to the mission while highlighting the themes of sacrifice, trust, and human resilience. Mann's purpose in the narrative is to exemplify the challenges and ethical dilemmas faced by humanity in its quest for survival and exploration. His actions force the crew to confront not only the immediate physical dangers but also the philosophical and moral questions posed by their mission. Through this conflict, the characters, particularly Cooper, are pushed to reaffirm their convictions and the altruistic motivations behind their journey. Mann's antagonism, therefore, is essential in advancing the plot and deepening the film's thematic concerns, proving once again that in Nolan's cinema, antagonists are fundamental to the narrative's development and its thematic richness.

Christopher Nolan's antagonists are masterfully crafted to serve a purpose far beyond mere opposition; they are essential drivers of the narrative and thematic exploration. Through complex characters like The Joker, Mal, and Dr. Mann, Nolan utilizes antagonists to challenge his protagonists in deeply personal and existential ways, compelling them to evolve and adapt. These antagonists catalyze the narrative progression and enrich the story's exploration of philosophical and moral dilemmas, demonstrating Nolan's skill in creating films that are not only visually stunning but also intellectually and emotionally engaging.

Chapter 4: Pre-production Essentials

Storyboarding: Nolan's approach to visualizing scenes.

Christopher Nolan's approach to filmmaking is characterized by meticulous planning and visual storytelling, with storyboarding playing a crucial role in his process. Nolan's method of storyboarding is not merely a preliminary step but a fundamental aspect of his narrative construction, enabling him to visualize complex scenes and sequences before they are brought to life on screen. This technique allows Nolan to explore the spatial and temporal dimensions of his narratives, ensuring that each frame contributes to the overall story and thematic exploration. For Nolan, storyboarding is an essential tool in achieving the visual coherence and thematic depth that his films are known for. His use of storyboarding in "Inception" (2010) exemplifies this approach. The film's intricate plot, which involves dreams within dreams, required a precise visual language to differentiate between various layers of reality. Nolan's detailed storyboards helped in designing the distinct visual cues for each dream level, facilitating a seamless transition between these layers and aiding audience comprehension. This level of visual planning was crucial in realizing the film's ambitious sequences, such as the rotating hallway fight scene, which combined practical effects with complex choreography. Through storyboarding, Nolan was able to pre-visualize the sequence in great detail, allowing for meticulous preparation and coordination that ensured the scene's success both technically and narratively.

Storyboarding also plays a pivotal role in Nolan's manipulation of time and space, a recurring theme in his work. "Interstellar" (2014), with its depiction of space travel, wormholes, and distant planets, presented unique challenges in visual storytelling. Nolan's storyboards were instrumental in conceptualizing the film's groundbreaking visual effects, particularly in scenes involving the depiction of a black hole and the time dilation experienced by the characters. The precision in visualizing these scientific concepts through storyboarding allowed Nolan to work closely with visual effects teams to create imagery that was not only spectacular but also grounded in theoretical physics. This collaboration between Nolan's vision and the expertise of scientists and visual effects artists was facilitated by the detailed storyboards, ensuring that the film's portrayal of space remained as accurate as possible while still serving the story's emotional core. The storyboarding process thus became a bridge between Nolan's narrative ambitions and the technical execution required to bring his vision to the screen.

Furthermore, Nolan's approach to storyboarding is reflective of his overall filmmaking philosophy, which emphasizes practical effects and real locations over digital alternatives. In "Dunkirk" (2017), Nolan's use of storyboarding was crucial in planning the film's extensive practical effects and action sequences. The storyboards allowed Nolan to map out the film's complex aerial dogfights, the evacuation sequences on the beaches, and the claustrophobic scenes aboard the naval vessels, ensuring that each element was cohesively integrated into the film's narrative structure. This meticulous planning was essential in coordinating the live-action sequences, many of which involved hundreds of extras, practical explosions, and vintage aircraft. By visualizing these sequences through storyboarding, Nolan was able to achieve a level of realism and immersion that significantly enhanced the film's impact. The storyboards not only guided the technical aspects of these sequences but also ensured that they remained true to the historical events the film depicts, reinforcing Nolan's commitment to authenticity.

Christopher Nolan's use of storyboarding is a testament to his belief in the power of visual storytelling. Through this process, Nolan is able to meticulously plan and execute his vision, ensuring that each scene aligns with the narrative's larger thematic concerns. His approach to storyboarding exemplifies his overall filmmaking style, characterized by a synergy between narrative ambition and technical precision. Whether exploring the depths of the subconscious in "Inception," the vastness of space in "Interstellar," or the chaos of war in "Dunkirk," Nolan's storyboards are a critical tool in translating complex concepts into compelling cinematic experiences. This methodical approach to visualizing scenes underscores Nolan's status as a master filmmaker, whose works continue to push the boundaries of the medium both narratively and visually.

Planning and research: The role of meticulous pre-production in Nolan's films.

Christopher Nolan's filmmaking process is distinguished by an unwavering commitment to meticulous planning and in-depth research, crucial elements that lay the groundwork for the realization of his cinematic visions. This rigorous approach to pre-production is evident across his diverse body of work, allowing Nolan to seamlessly blend complex narratives with groundbreaking visual storytelling. In "Inception" (2010), a film that explores the intricacies of dreams within dreams, Nolan's dedication to planning and research was paramount. The concept of navigating and manipulating the subconscious required a profound understanding of psychological theories and dream logic. Nolan and his team delved into research on the architecture of the mind, consulting with neuroscientists and psychologists to create a believable dream world with its own set of rules. This foundational work was critical in developing the film's unique narrative structure and visual language, enabling the creation of sequences that were both visually captivating and narratively coherent. The meticulous pre-production phase ensured that "Inception's" complex ideas were presented in a way that was accessible and engaging to audiences, demonstrating Nolan's ability to transform abstract concepts into compelling cinematic experiences.

Nolan's insistence on thorough planning and research is also manifest in his approach to historical and practical authenticity, as seen in "Dunkirk" (2017). Prior to filming, Nolan immersed himself in the history of the Dunkirk evacuation during World War II, studying firsthand accounts, historical documents, and consulting with historians to ensure the film's accuracy. This dedication extended to the practical aspects of the film's production, with Nolan opting to shoot on location and use period-correct planes and boats, some of which had participated in the actual evacuation. The extensive research and planning facilitated a filming process that captured the harrowing reality of the event, with minimal reliance on CGI. This authentic portrayal was instrumental in conveying the urgency, despair, and, ultimately, the hope of the Dunkirk evacuation, showcasing Nolan's commitment to respecting historical truth while delivering a powerful cinematic narrative.

Moreover, Nolan's methodical pre-production process plays a critical role in the logistical execution of his films, particularly those featuring elaborate set pieces and practical effects. "The Dark Knight" trilogy exemplifies how Nolan's penchant for realism and practical effects was realized through detailed planning. For instance, the destruction of the Gotham General Hospital in "The Dark Knight" (2008) and the mid-air plane hijacking in "The Dark Knight Rises" (2012) were achieved through intricate planning and precision, ensuring safety while maximizing visual impact. This approach required exhaustive research into the mechanics of the stunts, coordination with experts in various fields, and careful choreography to meld these ambitious practical effects seamlessly into the story. By investing in such detailed pre-production, Nolan ensures that each set piece not only serves the narrative but also enhances the film's overall authenticity and immersive quality.

Christopher Nolan's commitment to meticulous planning and extensive research in the pre-production phase of his films underscores his dedication to crafting immersive and intellectually engaging cinematic experiences. Whether delving into the psychological depths of the human subconscious, honoring the complexities of historical events, or orchestrating large-scale practical effects, Nolan's rigorous approach ensures that his ambitious visions are realized with integrity and precision. This commitment not only distinguishes Nolan as a filmmaker but also elevates the standard for cinematic storytelling, blending complex narratives with unparalleled visual and thematic depth.

Through his methodical preparation, Nolan challenges both the audience and the medium itself, pushing the boundaries of what cinema can achieve.

Casting: Strategies behind choosing the right actors for character-driven storytelling.

Christopher Nolan's approach to casting is as meticulous and deliberate as his narrative construction and visual storytelling. He has a keen eye for choosing actors who can bring depth, nuance, and authenticity to their roles, which is paramount in character-driven storytelling. Nolan's casting strategies are not merely about selecting individuals based on their star power but involve a deep understanding of the characters' complexities and how an actor's persona and skill set can enhance the narrative. This process is evident in his consistent collaboration with certain actors across multiple projects, suggesting a level of trust and mutual understanding that contributes to the films' success. For instance, Michael Caine has become a recurring figure in Nolan's films, appearing in roles that vary greatly in terms of complexity and screen time. Caine's versatile acting skills and his ability to convey warmth, wisdom, or moral ambiguity with subtlety align perfectly with Nolan's need for multi-dimensional characters. This partnership highlights how Nolan's casting decisions are strategic and character-focused, aiming to enrich the narrative through performances that resonate with authenticity and emotional depth.

Nolan's strategy in casting also involves identifying actors who can embody the thematic essence of the film and contribute to its larger narrative ambitions. In "The Dark Knight" (2008), the casting of Heath Ledger as The Joker was initially met with skepticism. However, Nolan saw in Ledger a profound ability to inhabit the character's anarchic spirit and psychological complexity. Ledger's transformative performance not only defied expectations but also became central to the film's exploration of chaos, morality, and the duality of heroism and villainy. Similarly, in "Inception" (2010), Leonardo DiCaprio was cast as Dom Cobb, a role that demanded a delicate balance between the character's internal turmoil and his professional expertise as a dream extractor. DiCaprio's nuanced portrayal of Cobb's vulnerability, guilt, and determination added layers to the film's exploration of memory, loss, and redemption. Nolan's ability to foresee how an actor can encapsulate the thematic depth of the story underscores his strategic approach to casting, ensuring that performances enhance both character development and thematic exploration.

In "Interstellar" (2014), Nolan's casting choices further illustrate his strategy of aligning actors with the film's emotional and intellectual demands. Matthew McConaughey, cast as Cooper, brought a blend of everyman relatability and profound emotional depth to the role, embodying the film's themes of love, sacrifice, and the quest for knowledge. McConaughey's performance grounded the film's high-concept science fiction elements in human experience, making the story accessible and emotionally compelling. Anne Hathaway, Jessica Chastain, and the rest of the ensemble were similarly chosen for their ability to convey the film's complex emotional and philosophical questions through genuine, impactful performances. Nolan's casting strategy for "Interstellar" emphasized emotional authenticity, ensuring that the human element remained at the forefront of this epic space exploration narrative.

Christopher Nolan's approach to casting is a critical component of his filmmaking process, reflecting a thoughtful strategy that prioritizes character depth and narrative cohesion. By choosing actors who can fully embody their characters' complexities and resonate with the film's thematic concerns, Nolan ensures that his films engage audiences on multiple levels. This careful alignment of actors with roles enhances the storytelling, allowing for a richer, more immersive cinematic experience. Nolan's casting decisions not only contribute to the success of his films but also demonstrate his broader commitment to creating cinema that is intellectually stimulating and emotionally resonant. Through his strategic casting choices, Nolan continues to elevate the art of character-driven storytelling, affirming the indispensable role of performance in bringing cinematic narratives to life.

Analysis of set design and location choice in establishing mood and theme.

The art of set design and the strategic choice of locations are central to Christopher Nolan's filmmaking, serving not just as backdrops for action but as integral components that establish mood, underscore themes, and enhance narrative depth. Nolan's approach to set design and location selection is characterized by a meticulous attention to detail and a profound understanding of how physical space can reflect and amplify character psychology, plot dynamics, and thematic exploration. In "Inception" (2010), the manipulation of physical space is both a narrative device and a thematic exploration, making set design and location choice crucial to the film's impact. The dream worlds created by the characters are visually distinct and thematically resonant, from the labyrinthine streets of the Paris dreamscape to the austere architecture of the fortress in the snow. These settings do more than provide a stage for the narrative; they reflect the inner worlds of the characters and the film's exploration of the subconscious. The Paris dreamscape, with its bending streets and impossible architecture, visually represents the film's central theme of the malleability of reality within dreams.

Nolan's choice to use practical effects for the folding city scene, building a physical set, underscores his commitment to grounding even the film's most fantastical elements in a tangible reality, thereby enhancing the mood of wonder and the theme of creation's power and peril.

Similarly, in "The Dark Knight" trilogy, Nolan's Gotham City evolves across the films, with set design and location choices reflecting the changing mood and themes of the series. In "Batman Begins" (2005), Gotham is depicted as a city overrun by crime and corruption, with the Narrows serving as a physical manifestation of the city's decay. The claustrophobic, maze-like design of the Narrows, coupled with the use of dark, saturated colors, establishes a mood of despair and highlights the theme of fear that runs through the film. As the trilogy progresses, Gotham's appearance shifts, mirroring the narrative developments and the characters' arcs. In "The Dark Knight" (2008), the cityscape is more open, yet it feels no less oppressive, reflecting the anarchic threat posed by the Joker. The choice of Chicago as a primary filming location for Gotham in this installment adds a layer of realism to the city, grounding the superhero story in a recognizable urban environment that enhances the film's exploration of justice, chaos, and moral ambiguity. By "The Dark Knight Rises" (2012), Gotham has become a character in its own right, with set design and locations reflecting the themes of revolution and redemption. The use of New York

City and Pittsburgh as locations adds to the sense of scale and realism, while specific sets, like the underground prison, symbolize the film's exploration of hope and resilience.

Nolan's "Interstellar" (2014) further exemplifies the critical role of set design and location in establishing mood and theme. The stark contrast between the dusty, dying Earth and the vast, unknown expanse of space serves as a visual metaphor for the film's exploration of human survival, environmental decay, and the quest for a new home. The design of the spacecraft and the barren landscapes of the alien planets are meticulously crafted to immerse the audience in the characters' journey, enhancing the themes of exploration, sacrifice, and love across dimensions. The choice of Iceland as a filming location for the alien planets, with its otherworldly landscapes, reinforces the film's mood of awe and isolation, highlighting the contrast between the familiar and the unknown.

Through his strategic use of set design and location choice, Christopher Nolan masterfully establishes mood and theme, creating immersive worlds that resonate with audiences. His films demonstrate a keen awareness of how physical space can reflect and enhance narrative and thematic concerns, proving that in cinema, the setting is much more than just a backdrop—it's a vital narrative force.

Chapter 5: Nolan's Directing Techniques

In-Camera magic: The philosophy behind practical effects.

Christopher Nolan's filmmaking philosophy is deeply rooted in the belief that cinema's magic lies in its ability to captivate and immerse audiences through the tangible reality of its visuals. This belief fundamentally underpins his preference for practical effects over digital alternatives, a choice that not only defines his aesthetic but also enhances the narrative authenticity and emotional engagement of his films. Nolan's commitment to practical effects is driven by a desire to create a more immediate and visceral connection between the audience and the film's world. By utilizing in-camera techniques, Nolan ensures that the action and environments seen on screen exist within a physical space, lending a weight and credibility to them that digital effects might not achieve. This approach is evident in the rotating hallway fight scene in "Inception" (2010), a sequence that exemplifies the effectiveness of practical effects in achieving a sense of physicality and immersion. Instead of relying on computer-generated imagery (CGI), Nolan and his team constructed a massive rotating set that allowed the actors to perform the gravity-defying stunts in real time. This not only heightened the realism of the sequence but also allowed the actors to fully inhabit their roles, reacting in genuine ways to the physical challenges of the scene. The result is a captivating piece of cinema that stands as a testament to the power of practical effects to engage audiences in the spectacle while maintaining a grounded sense of reality.

Nolan's philosophy extends beyond the desire for visual authenticity; it also encompasses a broader perspective on filmmaking as a craft and an art form. He views the use of practical effects as a means to preserve the integrity of the cinematic experience, a stance that reflects a respect for the medium's history and its physical nature. In "Dunkirk" (2017), Nolan applied this philosophy to the depiction of the historical evacuation of Allied troops during World War II, opting for real locations, period-accurate planes and ships, and practical stunts to recreate the events. This commitment to authenticity extended to filming on the actual beaches of Dunkirk, using practical effects to simulate combat, and even employing vintage aircraft for aerial scenes. The use of practical effects not only imbued the film with a palpable sense of realism but also honored the true story of Dunkirk by capturing the raw intensity and chaos of the evacuation. Nolan's approach underscores his belief that practical effects, coupled with traditional filmmaking techniques, can more effectively convey the emotional and historical weight of a story, creating an immersive and impactful viewing experience.

Moreover, Nolan's preference for practical effects over digital ones is not merely a technical choice but a narrative-driven decision. He believes that practical effects contribute to the storytelling process by grounding fantastical elements in a recognizably real world, thereby enhancing the suspension of disbelief among audiences. For example, in "The Dark Knight" (2008), the practical destruction of a full-sized hospital and the flipping of an 18-wheeler in the streets of Chicago were monumental feats that served to amplify the stakes of the narrative and the physicality of the film's world. These moments are not just impressive set pieces but integral parts of the story that reflect the characters' actions and the thematic depth of the film. By choosing practical effects, Nolan ensures that these pivotal scenes retain a sense of immediacy and consequence, reinforcing the themes of chaos and moral ambiguity that permeate the film. This integration of practical effects into the narrative fabric of his films demonstrates Nolan's holistic view of filmmaking, where every technical choice is made in service of enhancing the story and deepening the audience's emotional connection to the film.

Christopher Nolan's dedication to in-camera magic and practical effects is a defining aspect of his cinematic philosophy, reflecting a deep commitment to preserving the tactile essence of film. By favoring practical effects, Nolan not only challenges the norms of contemporary blockbuster filmmaking but also reaffirms cinema's power to awe and inspire through the artistry and craftsmanship of its creation. This approach results in films that are not only visually stunning and narratively compelling but also resonate with a sense of authenticity and immediacy rare in the digital age. Nolan's work stands as a testament to the enduring magic of practical effects in cinema, showcasing the unparalleled potential of traditional filmmaking techniques to captivate and engage audiences in an increasingly digital landscape.

Integrating CGI with practical effects: Maintaining authenticity.

Christopher Nolan's approach to filmmaking meticulously balances the integration of Computer-Generated Imagery (CGI) with practical effects, setting a benchmark in the industry for maintaining authenticity while exploiting the advancements in visual technology. Nolan's philosophy prioritizes the tangible and the real, using CGI not as a replacement for practical effects but as an enhancement that broadens the scope of what can be realistically depicted on screen. This harmonious integration is pivotal in creating immersive cinematic experiences that captivate audiences without sacrificing the grounded realism that is a hallmark of his films. A prime example of this approach can be seen in "Interstellar" (2014), where Nolan's ambition to authentically portray space travel, black holes, and distant galaxies necessitated a blend of practical sets and CGI. The film's depiction of the wormhole and the black hole, Gargantua, involved groundbreaking use of visual effects, informed by theoretical physics to ensure scientific plausibility. However, Nolan grounded these digital effects in the physical reality of the film's sets and locations, such as the cornfields and the interiors of the spacecraft, which were built as practical sets. This meticulous blending of CGI with practical elements allowed Nolan to create a visually stunning representation of space that felt both awe-inspiring and authentically tangible, reinforcing the film's themes of exploration, love, and the human spirit.

In "The Dark Knight" trilogy, Nolan's use of CGI to enhance practical effects demonstrates his commitment to maintaining authenticity while still delivering the spectacle expected of a superhero film. For instance, the Batmobile (Tumbler) chase scenes and the Batpod sequences were executed with practical stunts and real vehicles designed and built specifically for the films. CGI was judiciously used to enhance these sequences, removing safety rigs, and extending the Gotham cityscape, but the core of the action was captured in-camera. This approach ensured that the action sequences retained a visceral physicality and weight, making them more impactful and believable. Furthermore, the destruction of the Gotham General Hospital in "The Dark Knight" (2008) was a controlled demolition of a real building, with CGI used sparingly to augment the explosion and debris. Nolan's restraint in the use of

CGI, favoring practical effects wherever feasible, underscores his belief in the importance of physical presence and action in filmmaking. This strategy not only enhances the authenticity of the visual experience but also respects the audience's ability to discern the genuine from the artificial, deepening their engagement with the narrative and characters.

Moreover, Nolan's innovative integration of CGI and practical effects is evident in "Inception" (2010), particularly in the creation of the film's dreamscapes. While the film is renowned for its extensive use of practical effects, such as the rotating hallway and the Paris folding city sequence, CGI played a crucial role in realizing some of its more fantastical elements. For example, the visual representation of Limbo required the seamless blending of digital effects with real-world locations to create a hauntingly desolate dreamscape that reflects the characters' subconscious. By anchoring these digitally-enhanced scenes in the physicality of the actors' performances and practical sets, Nolan ensures that even the most surreal elements of the story maintain a grounding in reality. This careful balance between digital and practical methodologies allows "Inception" to explore complex narrative themes within a visually coherent and believable world, showcasing Nolan's skill in using CGI to expand the possibilities of storytelling without detracting from the film's authenticity.

Christopher Nolan's mastery in integrating CGI with practical effects to maintain authenticity in his films exemplifies his nuanced understanding of visual storytelling. His approach respects the audience's desire for realism, ensuring that the use of digital effects serves the narrative and enhances the emotional impact of the story, rather than overshadowing it. Through films like "Interstellar," "The Dark Knight" trilogy, and "Inception," Nolan demonstrates that the judicious use of CGI, when combined with a solid foundation of practical effects and real-world elements, can create cinematic experiences that are both visually spectacular and deeply grounded in reality. This methodology not only sets Nolan apart as a filmmaker but also contributes to the ongoing dialogue about the role of technology in cinema, advocating for a balanced approach that values the art of filmmaking as much as the science behind it.

Nolan's unique approaches to directing, including his hands-on style and rehearsals.

Christopher Nolan is renowned for his unique approach to directing, characterized by a hands-on style that emphasizes meticulous planning, extensive rehearsals, and a profound engagement with every aspect of the filmmaking process. Nolan's hands-on approach is evident in his preference for shooting on film, a choice that speaks to his dedication to the craft of cinema and his belief in the superior visual quality and texture that film offers. This commitment to traditional filmmaking techniques extends to his preference for practical effects over CGI, real locations over green screens, and the use of IMAX cameras to capture expansive vistas and intricate action sequences. Nolan's involvement in these technical decisions underscores his hands-on approach, ensuring that the technological aspects of his films serve the narrative and thematic ambitions. Moreover, Nolan's hands-on style is not limited to technical aspects; it permeates his interaction with actors and crew, fostering a collaborative environment that encourages creativity and innovation. By being actively involved in all stages of production, from pre-production planning and location scouting to post-production editing and sound design, Nolan maintains a cohesive vision for his films, ensuring that each element aligns with his storytelling objectives.

Rehearsals play a crucial role in Nolan's directing approach, allowing him to explore character dynamics, fine-tune performances, and experiment with different interpretations of the script. Unlike directors who might limit rehearsals to save time or budget, Nolan views them as an essential part of the creative process, providing a space for actors to delve deeper into their roles and for Nolan to refine the film's narrative flow. This emphasis on rehearsals is particularly important given the complexity of Nolan's films, which often involve intricate plots, non-linear storytelling, and sophisticated themes. Through rehearsals, Nolan ensures that his actors are not only comfortable with the technical demands of their roles but also fully understand the narrative and thematic context of their performances. This collaborative process between Nolan and his actors helps to create layered, nuanced characters that resonate with audiences, enhancing the emotional and intellectual impact of his films.

Nolan's unique approach to directing also extends to his ability to balance large-scale, visually spectacular set pieces with intimate character moments, maintaining a focus on storytelling amidst the technical complexities of his films. This balance is achieved through Nolan's hands-on style and meticulous planning, which includes storyboarding every scene and working closely with the cinematography and production design teams to ensure that every visual element supports character development and narrative progression. Nolan's ability to manage the scale of his films, moving seamlessly between epic sequences and personal stories, demonstrates his skill as a storyteller and his commitment to cinema as a medium for exploring human experiences and emotions. This aspect of his directing approach is crucial in films like "Interstellar" and "Dunkirk," where the grandeur of the visuals never overshadows the human drama at the heart of the story.

Christopher Nolan's directing approach, characterized by his hands-on style, emphasis on rehearsals, and ability to weave complex narratives with visual spectacle, reflects his dedication to the craft of filmmaking. His methods not only ensure the technical excellence and narrative cohesion of his films but also foster a creative environment that encourages collaboration and innovation among cast and crew. Through his meticulous planning, commitment to practical filmmaking techniques, and focus on storytelling, Nolan has established himself as one of the most visionary directors of his generation, capable of creating films that are both intellectually stimulating and emotionally resonant. His unique approach to directing not only sets his films apart but also contributes to the ongoing evolution of cinema, challenging filmmakers and audiences alike to reimagine what is possible within the medium.

Techniques Nolan uses to guide performances and create iconic performances.

Christopher Nolan is distinguished not only by his innovative storytelling and visual mastery but also by his adeptness at guiding actors towards delivering iconic performances. His directorial techniques in this domain are characterized by a deep respect for the actor's craft, a collaborative spirit, and a precise vision for each character's role within the broader narrative landscape of his films. One of the key techniques Nolan employs is the provision of a detailed backstory and psychological profile for his characters, even if these details never explicitly make it to the screen. This approach allows actors to fully immerse themselves in their roles, understanding their characters' motivations, fears, and aspirations on a profound level. For instance, in preparing for the role of Bruce Wayne/Batman, Christian Bale was provided with rich contextual material that explored Wayne's psychological complexity—his traumas, his dual identity, and his moral dilemmas. This groundwork enabled Bale to deliver a nuanced performance that went beyond the typical superhero archetype, bringing depth and humanity to the character. Nolan's ability to convey the psychological and emotional dimensions of his characters in clear, compelling terms is instrumental in guiding actors to performances that resonate with audiences and critics alike.

Nolan's directorial technique also involves creating an environment that enables actors to give their best performances. He is known for his preference for shooting sequences in chronological order whenever possible, a practice that is relatively rare in the film industry due to its logistical and financial implications. However, Nolan believes that this approach helps actors develop a natural progression in their characters' emotional journeys, enhancing the authenticity and continuity of their performances. This was particularly evident in

"Memento" (2000), where the narrative's reverse chronological order posed unique challenges for Guy Pearce, who portrayed the lead character, Leonard Shelby. By filming the scenes in sequence, Nolan provided Pearce with the ability to genuinely experience Leonard's confusion and disorientation, grounding his performance in the character's reality. This meticulous attention to the actor's process underscores Nolan's commitment to the craft of performance, fostering a space where actors can deeply connect with their characters and the story's emotional arc.

Furthermore, Nolan is renowned for his ability to balance the demands of high-concept, visually complex films with the need for emotionally grounded, relatable performances. He achieves this through meticulous pre-production planning and by fostering close, collaborative relationships with his actors, encouraging them to contribute their insights and ideas about their characters. This collaborative atmosphere ensures that the actors' performances are tightly integrated with the film's visual and thematic elements, creating a cohesive cinematic experience. In "Inception," for instance, Nolan worked closely with Leonardo DiCaprio to shape the character of Dom Cobb, a thief who infiltrates dreams. DiCaprio's input was crucial in developing Cobb's emotional depth, particularly regarding his guilt and longing for his family, which became central to the film's narrative and emotional resonance. Nolan's openness to collaboration not only enriches the characters and the story but also empowers actors to deliver performances that are both impactful and iconic.

Christopher Nolan's success in eliciting iconic performances from his actors lies in his detailed character development, supportive directorial environment, and collaborative approach. By investing in the psychological complexity of his characters, ensuring continuity in their emotional journeys, and integrating performances with the film's broader narrative and visual scheme, Nolan has guided actors towards some of the most memorable roles in contemporary cinema. His techniques underscore a profound respect for the art of acting and a deep understanding of its role in storytelling, affirming his status as a director who draws out the best in his collaborators. Through these methods, Nolan continues to contribute to the creation of film performances that endure in the collective memory of audiences, enriching the cinematic landscape with characters that resonate with authenticity and emotional depth.

Nolan's approach to visual composition and movement within a scene.

Christopher Nolan's approach to visual composition and movement within a scene is a testament to his mastery of the cinematic form, demonstrating a keen understanding of how visual elements can be harnessed to enhance narrative depth and emotional impact. One of Nolan's signature techniques is his use of the camera to create dynamic spatial relationships within the frame, adding layers of meaning to the narrative and deepening the audience's engagement with the story. He often employs wide shots and sweeping camera movements to establish the scope and scale of the film's setting, while also using these visual strategies to reflect the internal states of his characters. For example, in "Interstellar," Nolan uses the vastness of space to visually represent the emotional distance between the protagonist, Cooper, and his children back on Earth. The expansive shots of galaxies and celestial bodies not only serve to underscore the film's themes of exploration and isolation but also mirror Cooper's personal journey and the sacrifices he makes. Similarly, in "Inception," Nolan's use of architectural spaces and the manipulation of physical laws within the dream sequences provides a visual metaphor for the characters' psychological landscapes and the fluid nature of reality. Through careful composition and movement, Nolan is able to convey complex ideas and emotions, making the visual aspect of his films an integral part of the storytelling process.

Nolan's attention to visual composition also extends to his innovative use of framing and perspective to convey thematic elements and character perspectives. He strategically employs tight close-ups,

POV shots, and unconventional angles to draw the audience closer to the characters, allowing for a more intimate connection with their experiences and dilemmas. In "The Dark Knight," Nolan uses such techniques to explore the duality of Batman and the Joker, framing their confrontations in a way that emphasizes the philosophical battle between order and chaos. The deliberate composition of these scenes, coupled with the dynamic movement between characters, serves to heighten the tension and underscore the moral ambiguities at the heart of the film. Nolan's ability to use visual composition and movement to reflect the thematic content of his films demonstrates his skill in visual storytelling, where every shot is meticulously crafted to contribute to the narrative's overall impact.

Moreover, Nolan's directional approach is characterized by his innovative use of temporal and spatial movement within scenes to create a unique cinematic language. This is most evident in his manipulation of time as a narrative device, a theme that recurs throughout his filmography. Nolan crafts scenes that play with temporal progression, using editing, camera movement, and visual cues to disrupt linear narrative structures. This technique not only challenges conventional storytelling but also deepens the viewer's engagement with the narrative, as seen in "Memento," where the reverse chronological order of scenes forces the audience to piece together the protagonist's fragmented memory. Nolan's command of visual composition and movement is instrumental in conveying the disorienting experience of memory loss, making the audience active participants in unraveling the story. This interplay between visual technique and narrative structure is a hallmark of Nolan's directorial style, showcasing his ability to merge form and content in innovative ways.

Christopher Nolan's approach to visual composition and movement within a scene reflects a profound understanding of cinema's power to convey complex narratives and evoke deep emotional responses. His meticulous attention to framing, perspective, and the dynamic use of camera movement allows for a richly layered visual experience that complements and enhances the storytelling. By integrating visual techniques with narrative and thematic elements, Nolan creates cinematic works that are not only visually stunning but also intellectually and emotionally resonant. His innovative use of visual composition and movement underscores his status as a visionary filmmaker, whose works continue to push the boundaries of the medium and inspire audiences and filmmakers alike.

The integration of blocking with storytelling to enhance narrative impact.

Christopher Nolan's directorial prowess is vividly showcased through his integration of blocking with storytelling, a technique that greatly enhances the narrative impact of his films. Blocking, the precise staging of actors within a scene, is not merely a matter of aesthetics for Nolan but a deliberate choice that deepens the audience's understanding of character dynamics, plot developments, and thematic undercurrents. Nolan utilizes blocking to visually represent relationships, power dynamics, and internal conflicts, thus enriching the narrative without the need for expository dialogue. In "The Dark Knight" (2008), Nolan's use of blocking during the interrogation scene between Batman and the Joker exemplifies this approach. The physical positioning of the characters within the confined space, their movements, and the distance between them are carefully choreographed to reflect the shifting power dynamic and the intense psychological battle unfolding. As the Joker's manipulation intensifies, the physical closeness between the characters varies, visually accentuating the Joker's control over the conversation and, by extension, over Gotham. This scene demonstrates how Nolan's strategic use of blocking underscores the thematic exploration of chaos and order, while also providing insight into the characters' psychological states.

Similarly, in "Inception" (2010), Nolan's innovative approach to blocking is integral to conveying the complex layers of the film's narrative structure and the characters' emotional journeys. The dream sequences, which form the core of the film's plot, utilize blocking to differentiate between the various levels of the subconscious. For instance, the synchronized movements of characters across different dream layers not only serve to orient the audience within the film's intricate plot but also highlight the characters' interconnectedness and reliance on each other. The physical arrangement of the characters within these layers—often in protective stances or formations—visually reinforces their collective endeavor and the stakes involved. Moreover, Nolan's blocking in these sequences subtly reflects the themes of inception and extraction, with characters navigating the physical spaces of the dream worlds in ways that mirror their manipulation of the dreamer's subconscious. Through such careful staging, Nolan ensures that blocking is not just a technical aspect of filmmaking but a narrative tool that enhances the storytelling and deepens the audience's engagement with the film.

Nolan's mastery of blocking as a narrative device is also evident in "Interstellar" (2014), where the spatial relationships between characters are used to underscore the film's exploration of time, space, and human connection. The physical separation between Cooper and his daughter, Murph, is a recurring visual motif that eloquently captures the emotional distance and the passage of time. Nolan employs blocking to poignantly illustrate their separation and eventual reunion, using physical space within the frame to reflect the characters' emotional arcs and the overarching theme of love transcending time and space. The staging of the characters within the vast, unfamiliar landscapes of the different planets they visit further emphasizes their isolation and vulnerability, reinforcing the film's themes of exploration, survival, and the search for home. Through these examples, it is evident that Nolan's strategic use of blocking is a powerful storytelling technique that significantly contributes to the narrative impact of his films.

In essence, Christopher Nolan's integration of blocking with storytelling is a testament to his holistic approach to filmmaking, where every element is meticulously crafted to serve the narrative. By employing blocking as a tool to visually communicate character relationships, emotional states, and thematic concerns, Nolan elevates the narrative impact of his films. This technique not only enhances the visual storytelling but also invites the audience to engage more deeply with the narrative, providing a richer, more immersive cinematic experience. Nolan's thoughtful use of blocking underscores his commitment to storytelling that is both visually compelling and emotionally resonant, solidifying his reputation as a filmmaker who masterfully blends form and content.

Detailed scene analysis: Exploring the staging of key scenes in Nolan's films.

Christopher Nolan's nuanced approach to scene composition and staging is brilliantly exemplified in the climax of "The Dark Knight Rises" (2012), where Batman confronts Bane for the final time. Unlike their first encounter in the sewers, which highlighted Batman's physical inferiority to Bane, the climactic fight is staged amidst the chaos of Gotham's streets, symbolizing not just a battle between hero and villain, but a fight for the soul of Gotham. The staging here, in broad daylight, contrasts sharply with the darkness of their first fight, reflecting Batman's journey back from despair and his reclaimed strength. The spatial arrangement of the characters, with Batman now confronting Bane head-on, surrounded by the citizens of Gotham, signifies Batman's role as Gotham's protector and the city's reawakened hope. The strategic positioning of Gotham's police force, led by Commissioner Gordon, and the freed prisoners, emphasizes the thematic undercurrent of unity and redemption. This scene's staging and composition underscore the narrative's climax, where the physical battle between Batman and Bane mirrors the ideological battle that has raged throughout the trilogy. Nolan's careful orchestration of this scene amplifies its impact, making it a defining moment that captures the trilogy's exploration of heroism, sacrifice, and the potential for redemption.

A detailed scene analysis from "Inception" — the Paris café explosion sequence — exemplifies Nolan's skill in using staging to amplify the emotional and psychological impact of a scene. In this sequence, Cobb introduces Ariadne to the construct of dream manipulation, culminating in the dramatic visual of the café environment exploding around them as time slows. The staging here is crucial; the characters are positioned centrally, calm amidst the chaos, highlighting their control within the dream world. This moment visually represents the core themes of "Inception": the manipulation of reality and the fine line between the dream world and waking life. The debris floating around them, captured with minimal CGI and practical effects, emphasizes the tangibility of the dream space, inviting the audience to question the nature of reality. The placement of characters and the slow-motion explosion serve not just as a spectacle but as a narrative device, illustrating the power of the subconscious mind and setting the tone for the exploration of dreams within the film.

Another striking example of Nolan's staging to enhance narrative impact is seen in "Batman Begins" (2005), particularly in the sequence where Bruce Wayne discovers the Batcave for the first time. This moment is pivotal, not just for the character's development but also for the thematic foundation of the trilogy. Nolan stages this discovery with a keen sense of spatial storytelling; Bruce's descent into the cave is both a literal and metaphorical journey into the depths of his own psyche and the inception of his transformation into Batman. The use of natural lighting, or rather the lack thereof, in this scene, emphasizes the cave's symbolism as the dark, unexplored parts of Bruce's mind where fear and determination reside. The staging of this scene—with Bruce standing in the midst of an uncharted territory, enveloped by darkness and the fluttering of bats—visually represents his acceptance of fear and his decision to embody the persona of Batman to fight the corruption in Gotham. This moment of realization and acceptance is a masterclass in using physical space and character positioning to underscore a character's internal journey and the thematic motifs of fear, identity, and rebirth that recur throughout Nolan's trilogy.

In "Interstellar," the docking sequence stands as a testament to Nolan's ability to combine technical prowess with narrative depth through staging. As the Endurance spins out of control near the wormhole, Cooper's decision to attempt a manual docking is a defining moment of human courage and determination in the face of insurmountable odds. The staging of this sequence, with the spacecraft set against the vastness of space, accentuates the isolation and peril faced by the characters. The rotation of the camera, aligning with the spin of the spacecraft, immerses the audience in the dizzying, desperate attempt to connect the two ships. This scene encapsulates the film's themes of survival, sacrifice, and the relentless pursuit of hope amidst despair. Through precise staging and visual composition, Nolan elevates this sequence from a mere action set piece to a moment of profound emotional and thematic significance, underscoring the film's exploration of humanity's place in the universe and the bonds that tie us to one another and to our planet.

The funeral scene for Bruce Wayne in "The Dark Knight Rises" showcases Nolan's adeptness at using staging to convey complex emotional states and narrative shifts without relying heavily on dialogue. The scene is carefully composed to juxtapose the private grief of Alfred, Bruce's loyal butler, with the public mourning of Gotham for its fallen hero. The spatial separation of Alfred from the other attendees encapsulates his personal loss, distinct from the city's collective mourning. This staging choice highlights the intimate bond between Alfred and Bruce, underscoring the theme of personal sacrifice and the cost of being Batman. The somber mood, the restrained performances, and the visual focus on Alfred's solitary figure in the crowd serve to deepen the emotional resonance of the scene, illustrating Nolan's ability to use blocking and composition to enhance the narrative's emotional depth. The subsequent reveal of Bruce's survival and Alfred's realization at a café in Florence completes the narrative arc, bringing a sense of closure and peace to both characters. The staging of this final revelation, with Alfred's reaction framed in a medium shot to capture the subtlety of his emotions, showcases Nolan's skill in using visual composition to deliver powerful narrative resolutions.

Through these examples, it's evident that Christopher Nolan's strategic use of staging and scene composition is integral to his storytelling approach, allowing him to weave complex narratives that engage audiences both visually and emotionally. His careful consideration of character placement, lighting, and spatial dynamics within scenes not only enhances the visual appeal of his films but also deepens their thematic exploration, making Nolan a master of cinematic storytelling.

Chapter 6: Visual Style and Cinematography

Examination of Nolan's visual signature.

Christopher Nolan's visual style and cinematography are distinctive, marked by a synthesis of grandeur and precision that has become a hallmark of his cinematic oeuvre. His visual signature is characterized by its emphasis on practical effects, natural lighting, and the innovative use of IMAX cameras, all of which contribute to a sense of immersive realism and epic scope that is uniquely Nolan's. One of the most notable aspects of Nolan's visual style is his preference for shooting on film, particularly in the IMAX format, to capture the texture and depth of the visual field with unparalleled clarity and detail. This choice not only reflects Nolan's commitment to the aesthetic qualities of traditional filmmaking but also enhances the visual storytelling of his films. For instance, in "Interstellar" (2014), the use of IMAX cameras allowed Nolan to convey the vast, awe-inspiring expanse of space in a way that was both visually stunning and emotionally resonant. The film's depiction of celestial phenomena, such as wormholes and black holes, benefits from the high-resolution imagery that IMAX provides, bringing a level of detail and grandeur to the screen that deepens the audience's engagement with the narrative's themes of exploration and the human spirit. Nolan's adept use of these cameras, combined with his preference for practical effects, grounds the film's more fantastical elements in a tangible reality, making the vastness of space feel accessible and intimately connected to the characters' journey.

Moreover, Nolan's cinematographic technique is characterized by its dynamic movement and framing, which serve to underscore the thematic elements and emotional undercurrents of his narratives. His collaboration with cinematographers like Wally Pfister and Hoyte van Hoytema has produced some of the most visually compelling sequences in contemporary cinema, marked by their fluid camera work and innovative compositions. In "The Dark Knight" (2008), Nolan and Pfister employed a variety of camera movements to enhance the psychological tension and moral ambiguity at the heart of the film. The use of aerial shots, for instance, provides a god-like perspective on Gotham's chaos, reflecting the overarching themes of surveillance and control, while the tight close-ups of characters during key moments of confrontation create a claustrophobic intensity that heightens the emotional stakes. Nolan's careful consideration of framing and movement not only enriches the visual texture of his films but also serves as a narrative device, guiding the audience's attention and evoking a visceral response to the unfolding drama.

Nolan's visual style also extends to his meticulous attention to color and lighting, which play a significant role in establishing mood and atmosphere. Unlike directors who may rely heavily on post-production color grading to achieve a certain aesthetic, Nolan prefers to use natural lighting and practical sources to illuminate his scenes, contributing to the realism and authenticity that define his films. This approach is evident in "Dunkirk" (2017), where the natural light of the sun, the sea, and the sky combine to create a visually arresting backdrop that underscores the film's themes of time, survival, and the human cost of war. The desaturated color palette and the stark lighting conditions serve to strip away any sense of glorification from the wartime setting, presenting the events in a raw, unfiltered manner that aligns with Nolan's objective to immerse the audience in the harrowing reality of the Dunkirk evacuation. The visual style of "Dunkirk," with its emphasis on naturalism and authenticity, exemplifies Nolan's ability to use cinematography not just as a means of capturing action but as a tool for conveying deep thematic resonance.

Christopher Nolan's visual signature, a blend of grandiose scale and meticulous detail, reflects his profound understanding of cinema as a visual medium capable of conveying complex narratives and deep emotional truths. Through his innovative use of technology, dynamic camera work, and naturalistic approach to lighting and color, Nolan crafts cinematic experiences that are both intellectually engaging and visually breathtaking. His commitment to the aesthetic and technical aspects of filmmaking, combined with his narrative ambition, makes Nolan's visual style distinctive and impactful, solidifying his status as one of the most visionary directors of his generation.

His use of long takes and tracking shots.

Christopher Nolan's adept use of long takes and tracking shots stands as a testament to his commitment to creating immersive and emotionally engaging cinematic experiences. These techniques, which allow scenes to unfold in real-time without the interruption of cuts, serve not only to showcase Nolan's technical prowess but also to deepen the narrative impact of his films. Long takes are utilized by Nolan to build tension, develop character, and enhance the storytelling, creating a seamless flow that draws viewers deeper into the narrative world. In "Dunkirk" (2017), Nolan employs long takes to convey the relentless passage of time and the immediacy of the characters' experiences during the evacuation of Dunkirk. These extended shots immerse the audience in the palpable sense of urgency and desperation felt by the soldiers and civilians stranded on the beach. By allowing the camera to linger, Nolan captures the vast, desolate landscape of the beach and the sea, juxtaposed against the cramped, chaotic conditions aboard the rescue vessels. This technique amplifies the film's themes of survival and the indomitable human spirit in the face of overwhelming adversity. The long takes in "Dunkirk" not only serve a narrative function but also showcase Nolan's ability to create visually stunning tableaux that linger in the viewer's memory long after the film has ended.

Tracking shots, another hallmark of Nolan's directorial style, are expertly used to follow characters through dynamic environments, offering a continuous, fluid perspective that enhances the storytelling. In "Inception" (2010), Nolan's use of tracking shots during the dream sequences effectively conveys the labyrinthine complexity of the dreamscapes and the fluidity of movement within them. One memorable tracking shot follows the characters as they navigate a crowded marketplace in Mombasa, weaving through the chaos in a manner that mirrors the intricate layers of the film's plot. This technique not only heightens the tension of the scene but also visually represents the characters' journey through the convoluted architecture of the mind. Similarly, in "The Dark Knight" (2008), Nolan employs tracking shots to intensify the action sequences, such as the chase scene involving the Batpod. The camera moves with the Batpod, dynamically capturing its high-speed maneuvers through Gotham's streets, creating a visceral sense of speed and danger. These tracking shots not only add to the thrill of the chase but also underscore the film's exploration of justice and chaos, as Batman navigates the morally ambiguous landscape of Gotham.

Nolan's strategic use of long takes and tracking shots is not merely a stylistic choice but a reflection of his narrative intentions and thematic concerns. Through these techniques, he achieves a level of immersion and continuity that conventional shot-reverse-shot editing might disrupt. Long takes and tracking shots demand meticulous planning, precise choreography, and a deep understanding of the spatial dynamics within a scene. Nolan's mastery of these techniques is evident in the seamless integration of action, character development, and thematic exploration, creating moments that are both cinematically breathtaking and narratively compelling. For example, "Interstellar" (2014) utilizes long takes and tracking shots to underscore the emotional depth of the characters' journey through space and time. These shots capture the awe-inspiring beauty of the cosmos while grounding the story in the personal sacrifices and connections that drive the characters. The continuous flow of the camera through the vastness of space parallels the characters' emotional odyssey, reinforcing the film's themes of love, loss, and the quest for knowledge.

Christopher Nolan's use of long takes and tracking shots illustrates his innovative approach to filmmaking, where technical execution and narrative expression are intricately intertwined. By employing these techniques with purpose and precision, Nolan not only challenges the conventions of cinematic storytelling but also enhances the viewer's engagement with the film. Through his skillful manipulation of time and space within a continuous shot, Nolan invites audiences to fully immerse themselves in the worlds he creates, experiencing the narrative's emotional and thematic depth without interruption. His ability to orchestrate complex sequences using long takes and tracking shots cements his reputation as a filmmaker who pushes the boundaries of the medium, offering audiences a uniquely captivating cinematic experience.

Use of IMAX to achieve visual grandeur.

Christopher Nolan's pioneering use of IMAX technology has revolutionized the cinematic experience, showcasing his commitment to achieving visual grandeur and immersing audiences in the narrative world of his films. Nolan's advocacy for and utilization of IMAX film cameras underscore his belief in the superiority of the format's resolution, color depth, and scale, particularly for scenes requiring expansive visual storytelling. The use of IMAX in "The Dark Knight" (2008) marked a significant turning point in commercial cinema, as Nolan became one of the first filmmakers to integrate IMAX footage within a major feature film, blending the format with traditional 35mm film to spectacular effect. The decision to shoot key sequences, such as the opening bank heist and the Hong Kong skyline scene, in IMAX was driven by Nolan's desire to enhance the visual impact and immersive quality of these moments. The larger film stock of IMAX, which offers unparalleled clarity and detail, allowed Nolan to capture the sweeping vistas and intricate action with a level of precision and grandeur unmatched by standard formats. This innovative approach not only elevated the aesthetic quality of the film but also deepened the audience's engagement with the story, proving that the use of IMAX could extend beyond documentary and short-form content to redefine narrative filmmaking.

Nolan's continued exploration and expansion of IMAX technology's narrative potential were further exemplified in "Interstellar" (2014), a film that pushed the boundaries of visual storytelling in its portrayal of space exploration and cosmic phenomena. Nolan's choice to shoot significant portions of the film in IMAX was instrumental in achieving the visual grandeur necessary to convey the story's epic scope and the vastness of the universe. The immersive quality of IMAX, with its high resolution and larger field of view, offered audiences a front-row seat to the cosmic wonders encountered by the characters, from the serpentine mountains of an alien planet to the mesmerizing visuals of a black hole. The use of practical effects, miniatures, and real locations, in combination with IMAX's superior visual capabilities, allowed Nolan to create a sense of authenticity and tangibility within the film's fantastical settings. This meticulous approach to visual storytelling, supported by the IMAX format, not only captivated audiences with its stunning imagery but also served to underscore the film's thematic explorations of time, love, and human endeavor.

In "Dunkirk" (2017), Nolan's use of IMAX cameras achieved a new level of visual and emotional immersion, capturing the harrowing experience of soldiers and civilians involved in the Dunkirk evacuation during World War II. Nolan's decision to shoot the film almost entirely in IMAX was driven by a desire to place the audience in the midst of the action, creating a visceral sense of presence on the beaches, in the skies, and on the seas where the events unfolded. The expansive aspect ratio of IMAX provided a panoramic view of the conflict, highlighting both the vast scale of the operation and the individual stories of courage and survival. The clarity and depth of the IMAX footage, combined with Nolan's masterful direction, resulted in a gripping portrayal of war that was both intimate and epic, offering a profound meditation on the nature of heroism and sacrifice. By leveraging the capabilities of IMAX to their fullest, Nolan was able to transcend traditional war film conventions, presenting a unique narrative experience that resonated deeply with audiences and critics alike.

Christopher Nolan's adept use of IMAX technology across his filmography has not only demonstrated the format's immense potential for enhancing narrative cinema but has also set a benchmark for visual storytelling. Through his innovative approach to filmmaking, Nolan has proven that IMAX can be a powerful tool for achieving visual grandeur while maintaining narrative depth and emotional resonance. His commitment to pushing the boundaries of what cinema can achieve visually, coupled with his ability to seamlessly integrate IMAX footage within complex narratives, has redefined audience expectations and expanded the possibilities of the cinematic experience. As Nolan continues to explore the capabilities of IMAX in his future projects, his work remains a testament to the enduring power of film as a medium for storytelling, inspiring filmmakers and audiences alike to reimagine the scope and impact of visual narrative art.

Lighting and color: Techniques to create mood and focus.

Christopher Nolan's approach to lighting and color in his films is as meticulously crafted as his narratives, serving as a crucial tool in creating mood, directing focus, and enhancing thematic depth. Nolan, along with his long-time collaborating cinematographers, such as Wally Pfister and Hoyte van Hoytema, employs lighting and color techniques that not only define the visual tone of his films but also subtly influence the audience's emotional and psychological engagement with the story. In "The Dark Knight" (2008), Nolan uses high-contrast lighting and a desaturated color palette to reflect Gotham's moral decay and the ambiguity of heroism. The interplay of shadows and light in the film, especially in scenes involving Batman, underscores the character's dual nature and the dichotomy between justice and vengeance. The use of cool blue tones in night scenes conveys a sense of isolation and introspection, while the sparing use of vibrant colors, like the Joker's green and purple, punctuates the chaos he brings to Gotham. This deliberate manipulation of lighting and color creates a mood that is tense and foreboding, perfectly encapsulating the film's exploration of good versus evil within the framework of a superhero narrative.

In "Interstellar" (2014), Nolan and van Hoytema utilize natural lighting and a broader color spectrum to differentiate between the vastness of space and the Earth's dying landscapes. The scenes set in space are characterized by the stark, unfiltered light of distant stars, which illuminates the spacecraft and its occupants in a way that feels both cold and mesmerizing, emphasizing the isolation and wonder of space exploration. The scenes on Earth, by contrast, employ warmer tones and softer lighting, highlighting the planet's natural beauty while underscoring the threat of its impending desolation. This contrast not only enhances the visual and emotional impact of the different settings but also reinforces the film's themes of home, survival, and the interconnectivity of the human experience across time and space. The careful application of lighting and color in "Interstellar" serves not just as a backdrop for the action but as a narrative device that deepens the audience's immersion in the story's epic journey.

Furthermore, Nolan's use of lighting and color to direct focus and guide the audience's attention is exemplified in "Inception" (2010). Through the strategic use of lighting, Nolan differentiates the various layers of the dream world, making it easier for audiences to navigate the film's complex narrative structure. The dream sequences employ a distinctive visual style that ranges from the sharply defined, high-contrast lighting of the cityscapes to the diffuse, ethereal glow of the snow-covered mountains. This variance in lighting not only serves to visually separate the different dream levels but also to evoke specific emotional responses associated with each layer's narrative significance. The color palette in "Inception" also plays a crucial role in setting the mood and focusing attention. The use of saturated colors in the dream worlds contrasts with the more muted tones of the waking world, highlighting the seductive allure of the dreams and the blurred lines between reality and illusion. Nolan's adept manipulation of lighting and color elevates the storytelling in "Inception," guiding the audience through the film's labyrinthine plot while enhancing the thematic exploration of memory, grief, and redemption.

Christopher Nolan's mastery in employing lighting and color techniques is a testament to his holistic approach to filmmaking, where every visual element is carefully considered to support the narrative and thematic objectives. By manipulating lighting and color to create mood, direct focus, and convey emotional and psychological nuances, Nolan demonstrates his ability to craft visually compelling films that resonate deeply with audiences. His innovative use of these techniques not only defines the aesthetic of his films but also enriches the cinematic experience, making Nolan's work a benchmark for visual storytelling in contemporary cinema.

Natural vs. artificial lighting in Nolan's films.

Christopher Nolan's films exhibit a nuanced interplay between natural and artificial lighting, a choice that significantly contributes to the mood, realism, and thematic depth of his cinematic universe. Nolan's preference for natural lighting is not merely an aesthetic decision but a narrative tool that enhances the authenticity of the visual storytelling and grounds even his most fantastical stories in a palpable reality. In "Dunkirk" (2017), Nolan's use of natural light serves to immerse the audience in the historical reality of the Dunkirk evacuation, capturing the stark, unvarnished truth of war. The reliance on daylight to illuminate the beaches, sea, and skies of Dunkirk brings a harsh clarity to the desperation and vulnerability of the soldiers and civilians awaiting rescue. This approach, coupled with the film's reliance on practical effects and real locations, reinforces the immediacy and intensity of the experience, allowing the audience to feel the sun's glare, the chill of the water, and the shadow of impending danger. The natural lighting in "Dunkirk" is contrasted with the artificial lighting used in confined spaces, such as the interiors of ships and the cockpit of a Spitfire, where strategic use of artificial light accentuates the claustrophobia and tension. Through this deliberate juxtaposition, Nolan uses lighting to enhance the film's emotional resonance, highlighting the human struggle for survival against the backdrop of a monumental historical event.

Conversely, in "Interstellar" (2014), Nolan creatively employs both natural and artificial lighting to differentiate between the earthbound scenes set in a near-future, ecologically deteriorating Earth and the scenes set in the vast expanse of space or on alien planets. The scenes on Earth are bathed in natural light, which imbues them with a sense of warmth and familiarity, albeit tinged with the sadness of a dying world. The use of natural lighting here serves to ground the science fiction narrative in a recognizable reality, enhancing the emotional connection between the audience and the characters' plight. In contrast, the scenes set in space or on other planets utilize a combination of natural and carefully crafted artificial lighting to convey the alien and often hostile environments the characters encounter. For example, the scenes on the water planet and the icy planet employ artificial lighting to create an otherworldly atmosphere that emphasizes the beauty and danger of these unexplored worlds. The lighting choices in these sequences not only serve to visually distinguish between the various settings of the film but also underscore the themes of exploration, isolation, and the search for a new home for humanity.

In "The Dark Knight" trilogy, Nolan's strategic use of lighting plays a pivotal role in exploring the duality of Batman's character and the moral ambiguity of Gotham City. The trilogy employs a mix of natural and artificial lighting to create a gritty, urban atmosphere that reflects the complexity and darkness of the city and its inhabitants. Daylight scenes often utilize natural light to expose Gotham in its raw, unfiltered state, highlighting the decay and corruption that Batman seeks to eradicate. Conversely, the night scenes, which are more prevalent and thematically significant, are lit with artificial sources that cast long shadows and create stark contrasts. This interplay of light and darkness mirrors the internal conflict of Bruce Wayne and the external chaos that Batman fights against. The use of artificial lighting in these scenes, especially the carefully orchestrated shadows, enhances the mysterious and fearsome persona of Batman, while also emphasizing the psychological depth and moral complexities of the character and his adversaries. Nolan's adept manipulation of lighting in the trilogy serves not only as a stylistic choice but as a narrative device that enriches the storytelling and deepens the thematic exploration of heroism, justice, and redemption.

Christopher Nolan's nuanced use of natural versus artificial lighting across his filmography demonstrates his deep understanding of lighting as a storytelling instrument. Whether capturing the harsh reality of war, the wonder of space exploration, or the moral ambiguity of a superhero's fight against crime, Nolan's lighting choices significantly enhance the narrative and thematic richness of his films. By balancing natural and artificial light, Nolan creates visually stunning and emotionally resonant cinematic experiences that draw audiences into the worlds he constructs. His deliberate and thoughtful approach to lighting underscores his commitment to filmmaking as a craft, where every technical decision serves the larger purpose of the narrative and contributes to the overall impact of the film. Through his masterful use of lighting, Nolan continues to push the boundaries of cinema, crafting stories that resonate with audiences long after the credits roll.

The Nolan Frame: Composition and Symmetry

The "Nolan Frame" refers to the distinctive way in which Christopher Nolan composes his shots, marked by meticulous composition and a keen use of symmetry that together create visually compelling scenes which are not only aesthetically pleasing but also deeply imbued with narrative significance. Nolan's frames often employ a symmetrical composition that serves to heighten the emotional impact of a scene, focus the viewer's attention, or underscore thematic elements within the narrative. This technique is evident across his body of work, from the tight, claustrophobic corridors of the "Tumbler" in "The Dark Knight" trilogy to the vast, expansive landscapes of "Interstellar." In "Inception," for instance, Nolan uses symmetry to visually represent the constructed nature of the dream worlds. The Paris folding sequence, where the city bends over itself, is a masterclass in symmetrical composition, creating a surreal yet ordered landscape that reflects the film's exploration of the architecture of the mind and the manipulation of perceived reality. This careful arrangement of visual elements within the frame not only captivates the viewer but also deepens the narrative, making the composition a critical aspect of storytelling in Nolan's films.

Furthermore, Nolan's use of the frame extends beyond mere symmetry to include the strategic placement of characters and objects within the composition, enhancing the visual storytelling and guiding the audience's focus. In "The Dark Knight," the framing of Batman against the backdrop of Gotham's skyline often employs symmetry to convey his dual role as guardian and outcast. The composition of these shots, with Batman centered and the city sprawling out on either side, visually encapsulates the isolation and burden of his fight against crime. Similarly, in "Interstellar," Nolan uses the frame to juxtapose the vastness of space with the intimacy of human emotion. One notable example is the shot of the Endurance spacecraft silhouetted against the enormous wave on the water planet, where the symmetry of the composition underscores the fragility and bravery of human exploration. Through such deliberate framing, Nolan emphasizes the themes of sacrifice, loneliness, and the enduring human spirit, crafting frames that are as emotionally resonant as they are visually striking.

Nolan's framing techniques also serve to create a sense of balance and harmony within the visual narrative, lending a timeless quality to his films. This is particularly evident in his use of architectural elements and landscapes to frame action and dialogue, creating compositions that are both dynamic and balanced. In "Dunkirk," the symmetry of the mole extending into the sea, with soldiers lined up on either side, serves as a powerful visual metaphor for the uncertainty and duality of war — hope and despair, courage and fear. The use of symmetry here not only heightens the visual impact of the scene but also reinforces the film's exploration of the human condition under extreme duress. Nolan's ability to meld visual symmetry with narrative depth ensures that each frame contributes to the overall storytelling, making his films a rich tapestry of visual and narrative artistry.

The "Nolan Frame" is thus a testament to Christopher Nolan's visionary approach to filmmaking, where composition and symmetry are not just aesthetic choices but integral components of the storytelling process. Through his innovative use of the frame, Nolan invites the audience to engage more deeply with the narrative, offering a visual experience that complements and enhances the thematic and emotional underpinnings of his stories. His meticulous attention to framing showcases his belief in the power of cinema to convey complex ideas and emotions in a visually intuitive manner, cementing his status as one of the most visually inventive directors of our time.

Chapter 7: Editing and Pacing: The Rhythm of a Nolan Film

Cross-Cutting and parallel action: Enhancing tension and drama.

Christopher Nolan's adept use of cross-cutting and parallel action stands as a defining element of his cinematic style, serving to enhance tension, drama, and narrative complexity across his filmography. This technique, which involves cutting between two or more scenes that occur simultaneously but in different locations, is masterfully employed by Nolan to build suspense, deepen thematic exploration, and connect disparate narrative threads into a cohesive whole. In "Inception" (2010), Nolan uses cross-cutting to extraordinary effect in the film's climax, where multiple layers of dreams unfold concurrently. The audience is navigated through a van plunging off a bridge in slow motion, a fight in a hotel devoid of gravity, and a shootout in a snowy mountain fortress, among other sequences. By cross-cutting between these parallel actions, Nolan not only heightens the suspense—given each layer operates within a different time dilation—but also underscores the film's thematic concerns regarding the nature of reality and the subconscious. This technique amplifies the drama by juxtaposing the calm with the chaotic, the slow with the fast-paced, effectively keeping viewers on the edge of their seats as the stakes escalate in each layer of the dream.

In "The Dark Knight" (2008), Nolan employs cross-cutting to enhance the film's central conflict between Batman and the Joker, creating a palpable sense of tension and moral ambiguity. A notable use of this technique is during the film's two ferry sequence, where Gotham's citizens must choose whether to destroy the other ferry to save themselves. Nolan cuts between the agonizing decision-making on both ferries, the Joker's anticipation of the chaos, and Batman's desperate attempt to stop him. This simultaneous action serves to not only ramp up the tension but also delve deep into the film's exploration of human nature, fear, and the choices that define us. By employing cross-cutting here, Nolan crafts a multi-layered narrative moment that is as philosophically engaging as it is suspenseful, showcasing his ability to weave complex narrative threads into a unified exploration of theme and character.

Moreover, Nolan's "Dunkirk" (2017) exemplifies his innovative use of cross-cutting to tell a nonlinear narrative that converges the experiences of characters on land, sea, and air. The film's structure relies heavily on cross-cutting between these three perspectives, each with its own timeline but all culminating in a singular dramatic event. This approach not only serves to build tension across the different fronts of the evacuation but also highlights the collective effort and shared destiny of the soldiers and civilians involved. The interweaving of these parallel actions, through precise and rhythmic cross-cutting, imbues the film with a sense of urgency and immediacy. Nolan's technique here emphasizes the fragmented yet interconnected nature of war experiences, providing a unique and immersive portrayal of the Dunkirk evacuation. The tension and drama are amplified by the audience's awareness of the converging timelines, creating a continuous crescendo of suspense leading to the climactic rescue.

Christopher Nolan's strategic use of cross-cutting and parallel action is a testament to his narrative ingenuity and his ability to create tension and drama that transcends the conventional storytelling framework. Through this technique, Nolan not only manages to maintain high levels of engagement and suspense but also deepens the thematic resonance of his films, connecting characters and events across different spatial and temporal dimensions. His masterful employment of cross-cutting enhances the cinematic experience, making his films not only visually captivating but also emotionally and intellectually stimulating. Nolan's approach to cross-cutting showcases his unique vision as a filmmaker, marking him as a contemporary master of weaving complex, multi-layered narratives that challenge and captivate audiences worldwide.

Pacing for mystery and revelation.

Christopher Nolan's filmmaking technique of "the slow reveal" is intricately linked with his handling of pacing, which masterfully orchestrates the unfolding of mystery and revelation within his narratives. This method is not merely about withholding information but is a deliberate narrative strategy that deepens engagement, builds suspense, and enhances the thematic complexity of his films. Nolan's adeptness at pacing allows him to carefully control the flow of information, making each revelation both surprising and inevitable in hindsight. A prime example of this technique can be seen in "Memento" (2000), a film that employs a reverse chronological narrative structure to mirror the protagonist's condition of short-term memory loss. By presenting the story's events in reverse, Nolan forces the audience to piece together the mystery in a manner akin to the protagonist, Leonard Shelby, experiencing the fragmentation and disorientation of his reality. The slow reveal of critical information across the narrative not only sustains the mystery but also amplifies the themes of memory, identity, and truth. As the pieces of the puzzle gradually come together, the audience is compelled to question the reliability of memory and perception, making the final revelation all the more impactful.

In "The Prestige" (2006), Nolan's use of pacing to orchestrate the slow reveal is central to the film's exploration of obsession, sacrifice, and the art of illusion. The narrative, structured around the rivalry between two magicians in late Victorian London, unfolds through a series of diaries within diaries, with each layer peeling back to reveal deeper truths about the characters and their obsessions. Nolan meticulously paces the film to parallel the three acts of a magic trick—the pledge, the turn, and the prestige—each act building upon the last to heighten anticipation and suspense. This structure serves to both engage the audience in the mystery of how the illusions are performed and to explore the deeper metaphorical implications of the magicians' pursuit of perfection. The slow reveal of the true cost of their obsessions is paced in such a way that the audience, like the magicians' audience within the film, is captivated by the spectacle while being drawn into a deeper contemplation of the nature of sacrifice and the desire for legacy. The pacing of the film, therefore, is not just a narrative device but a thematic one, reinforcing the film's meditation on the nature of art and the human cost of ambition.

Furthermore, in "Interstellar" (2014), Nolan employs a measured pacing to unfold the mysteries of space, time, and human connection. The film's exploration of these vast themes is supported by a pacing that allows for the gradual revelation of the scientific and emotional layers of the story. As the astronauts venture further into space, each discovery and setback is presented in a way that balances the advancement of the plot with moments of reflection, enabling the audience to ponder the implications of humanity's place in the universe and the bonds that tie us together across dimensions. The slow reveal of the film's central mysteries, including the nature of the beings behind the wormhole and the resolution of the father-daughter relationship at the heart of the story, is carefully calibrated to resonate emotionally with the audience while also satisfying their intellectual curiosity. Through this pacing, Nolan ensures that the revelations feel earned, resulting from the characters' journeys and the choices they make, rather than mere plot twists.

Christopher Nolan's mastery of "the slow reveal" through careful pacing is a hallmark of his directorial style, enriching his films with layers of mystery and revelation that invite audiences to actively engage with the narrative. By controlling the flow of information and the timing of key revelations, Nolan crafts films that are not only intellectually stimulating but also deeply emotional, offering a cinematic experience that lingers with the audience long after the film has ended. This approach to pacing, integral to Nolan's storytelling, showcases his ability to weave complex narratives that captivate and challenge audiences, cementing his status as one of the most innovative filmmakers of our time.

Time as a character: Manipulating pace to serve the narrative.

Christopher Nolan's films frequently personify time, not merely as a narrative backdrop but as an active, shaping force within his stories, often becoming as pivotal as any character. This personification is intricately tied to Nolan's manipulation of pacing, which he adeptly employs to serve and enhance the narrative structure of his films. By doing so, Nolan elevates time from a mere chronological sequence to a thematic element that directly influences the actions of characters and the unfolding of the plot. In "Interstellar" (2014), time's elasticity, especially as dictated by the theory of relativity, becomes a central narrative and emotional fulcrum. The pacing of the film, particularly in the scenes depicting the relativistic time dilation experienced by the astronauts as opposed to Earth's passage of time, profoundly impacts the characters' arcs and the storyline. Nolan meticulously uses pacing to underscore the heartbreaking implications of their time in space, where hours equate to years lost with loved ones on Earth. The slow reveal of the consequences of their journey across time zones serves to heighten the emotional stakes, making time itself a character that exerts a profound influence over the narrative's progression and the characters' destinies.

In "Dunkirk" (2017), Nolan again manipulates pacing to personify time, using it to structure the narrative through three interwoven timelines of land, sea, and air, which converge in a climactic moment of unity. The differing speeds at which time progresses across these stories—ranging from a week on the beach, to a day at sea, to an hour in the air—create a unique pacing that builds tension and anticipation. This approach not only reflects the chaotic, fragmented experience of war but also amplifies the suspense as the timelines draw closer together, culminating in the evacuation's peak moment. Through this manipulation of narrative pace, Nolan crafts a palpable sense of urgency and desperation, with time acting as both adversary and ally. The characters, whether aware of it or not, are racing against time—a race that imbues their actions with greater significance and the narrative with a relentless forward momentum.

Moreover, "Inception" (2010) showcases Nolan's fascination with time as a narrative device, employing it to craft a multi-layered story that explores the subjective nature of time within dreams. Here, Nolan uses pacing to differentiate the flow of time across various levels of the dream world, with each level experiencing time at an exponentially slower pace. This manipulation of time serves to amplify the tension and complexity of the heist, as characters navigate deeper into the subconscious, risking being trapped in limbo. The pacing of these sequences is critical, with cross-cutting between levels to maintain narrative cohesion and suspense, underscoring the urgency of their mission against the dilating time. Time, manipulated through pacing, becomes a character that challenges the protagonists, shaping their journey and the narrative's unfolding. The film's climax, masterfully paced to synchronize the kicks across dream levels, exemplifies Nolan's ability to weave time into the fabric of the story, making it a crucial element that drives the narrative forward.

Christopher Nolan's treatment of time as a character, manipulated through pacing to serve the narrative, is a testament to his innovative storytelling. Through films like "Interstellar," "Dunkirk," and "Inception," Nolan not only challenges audiences' perceptions of time but also uses its fluidity to deepen the narrative impact of his stories. By personifying time and intricately weaving it into the pacing of his films, Nolan crafts narratives that are as intellectually engaging as they are emotionally resonant. This unique approach not only underscores Nolan's mastery over the medium but also highlights the thematic richness and complexity of his work, firmly establishing him as one of the most visionary filmmakers of our time.

Scene analyses: Examining editing choices in "Memento" and "The Prestige."

In "Memento" (2000), Christopher Nolan's exploration of memory and identity is profoundly influenced by his innovative editing choices, which serve as the backbone of the film's narrative structure. The film's unique storytelling method, which interlaces color sequences proceeding in reverse chronological order with black-and-white sequences moving chronologically, challenges conventional narrative and editing techniques. This juxtaposition creates a disorienting yet compelling narrative experience that mirrors the protagonist, Leonard Shelby's, fragmented and unreliable memory. One pivotal scene that exemplifies Nolan's masterful editing is when Leonard burns the items of his wife, including her photograph. This scene is pivotal as it marks a moment of erasure, an attempt by Leonard to reset his quest for vengeance. The editing seamlessly transitions between Leonard's actions in the present and his recollections—or lack thereof—of the past, highlighting the cyclical nature of his quest and the futility of seeking closure when anchored to an unreliable memory. The use of jump cuts and cross-cutting in this scene not only serves to disorient the viewer but also to deepen the engagement with Leonard's psyche, effectively making the audience question the veracity of what they are witnessing. Nolan's editing choices in "Memento" do not merely serve the narrative; they enhance the film's thematic exploration of memory, identity, and the subjective nature of truth, showcasing his ability to intertwine narrative complexity with technical prowess.

"The Prestige" (2006), another Nolan masterpiece, utilizes editing not only to weave together a complex narrative spanning different timelines but also to reflect the film's central theme of obsession and the art of illusion. The editing intricately layers the film's narrative, moving between the past and present to reveal the depth of the rivalry between two magicians, Robert Angier and Alfred Borden. A standout scene that highlights Nolan's editing genius is the final act where the ultimate illusion, "The Prestige," is revealed. The editing pace accelerates as the film approaches this climax, cross-cutting between Borden in prison reading Angier's diary, Angier performing his final show, and Cutter discovering the water tanks containing Angier's clones. This rapid editing builds suspense and anticipation, drawing the audience deeper into the magicians' obsession. It's the revelation of Borden's twin and the implications of Angier's duplications where Nolan's editing choices shine, masterfully balancing the revelation and concealment of information. The technique of revealing information in a non-linear fashion, akin to the layers of a magic trick, allows Nolan to control the pacing of revelations, keeping the audience engaged and contributing to the film's thematic richness. Through these editing choices, Nolan explores the destructive nature of obsession, the cost of artistic perfection, and the thin line between genius and madness, making "The Prestige" not only a narrative about rivalry but also a meditation on the nature of human ambition and sacrifice.

In both "Memento" and "The Prestige," Christopher Nolan's editing choices are instrumental in crafting narratives that are as intellectually stimulating as they are emotionally resonant. Through the innovative structure of "Memento," Nolan challenges the audience's perception of memory and identity, using editing not just as a tool to tell a story but as a means to engage the audience in a deeper exploration of the film's themes. Similarly, in "The Prestige," the editing serves to enhance the film's exploration of obsession, sacrifice, and the cost of illusion, embedding the narrative with a complexity that invites multiple viewings. Nolan's editing techniques, characterized by their non-linear narrative structure, meticulous pacing, and strategic revelation of information, underscore his mastery of the medium. These choices not only contribute to the visual and narrative style of each film but also reinforce Nolan's reputation as a filmmaker who pushes the boundaries of conventional storytelling, using every element of the filmmaking process to deepen the thematic impact and audience engagement of his work.

Chapter 8: Soundtrack and Sound Design

The role of sound effects in Nolan's storytelling.

Christopher Nolan's storytelling is distinguished not just by its visual splendor but also by its intricate use of sound effects, which play a crucial role in deepening the narrative, enhancing thematic elements, and immersing the audience in the film's universe. Nolan, in collaboration with sound designers and editors, carefully crafts soundscapes that complement his storytelling, making sound effects an integral part of the narrative fabric. In "Interstellar" (2014), the sound effects are meticulously designed to convey the vastness and mystery of space, as well as the perilous nature of the astronauts' journey. The sounds of the spacecraft, from the hum of its engines to the eerie silence of space, serve to underscore the isolation and vulnerability of the characters. The stark contrast between the noisy interiors of the spacecraft and the silence of space highlights the film's exploration of human endeavors against the backdrop of the infinite universe. The sound effects in "Interstellar" not only create a realistic portrayal of space travel but also augment the film's emotional impact, especially in scenes that underscore the characters' desperation and determination. For example, the intense sound design during the docking sequence adds to the tension and urgency of the moment, making it one of the film's most memorable scenes.

In "Dunkirk" (2017), Nolan uses sound effects to create a visceral experience of war, employing them to not just accompany the visual spectacle but to place the audience in the midst of the action. The sounds of gunfire, explosions, and the roar of airplane engines are rendered with harrowing realism, contributing to the film's immersive quality. The sound design is particularly effective in conveying the omnipresent danger, from the sudden screech of Stuka dive bombers to the muffled underwater sounds that follow the sinking of a ship. These sound effects, combined with the film's minimal dialogue, demand the audience's full attention, drawing them deeper into the experience of the soldiers and civilians caught in the evacuation. The use of sound in "Dunkirk" is a testament to Nolan's understanding of its power to evoke visceral reactions, create tension, and communicate the chaos and fear of war without resorting to graphic violence.

Furthermore, Nolan's innovative use of sound effects in "The Dark Knight" (2008) serves to heighten the psychological tension and underscore the moral ambiguity at the heart of the film. The sound of the Joker's unsettling lip smacks, the echo of Batman's cape in the wind, and the visceral effects used during action sequences contribute to the film's dark and intense atmosphere. These sound effects are carefully juxtaposed with moments of silence to create a dynamic soundscape that reflects the internal and external conflicts of the characters. For example, the muffled sounds during the Joker's pencil trick scene amplify the shock of the moment, making the violence more impactful by focusing on the characters' reactions rather than the act itself. Nolan's use of sound effects in "The Dark Knight" not only enhances the storytelling but also contributes to the film's exploration of fear, chaos, and the thin line between heroism and vigilantism.

The role of sound effects in Christopher Nolan's films is multifaceted, serving not only to enhance the realism and immersive quality of his cinematic worlds but also to deepen the narrative and thematic richness of his stories. Through his thoughtful and innovative use of sound, Nolan demonstrates a profound understanding of its potential to influence the audience's emotional and psychological engagement with the film. His meticulous attention to sound design showcases his commitment to creating a sensory-rich cinematic experience that complements his complex narratives and visually stunning imagery. Nolan's films underscore the importance of sound effects in storytelling, proving that they are indispensable tools in the filmmaker's arsenal, capable of transforming the narrative landscape and elevating the cinematic experience.

The role of silence in Nolan's storytelling.

Christopher Nolan's storytelling is renowned for its complexity and depth, achieved not only through dialogue, visual effects, and music but also through his masterful use of silence. Within Nolan's cinematic universe, silence transcends its absence of sound to become a powerful narrative tool, shaping the audience's emotional response and enhancing the thematic weight of his films. This nuanced use of silence can profoundly impact the storytelling process, creating moments of tension, introspection, and revelation that linger with the audience long after the film has ended.

In "Dunkirk" (2017), Nolan's strategic use of silence is pivotal in conveying the harrowing reality of war and the raw emotion of survival. The film, which chronicles the evacuation of Allied soldiers during World War II, employs silence in stark contrast to the cacophony of battle and the roaring engines of planes and ships. These moments of silence, especially when soldiers are waiting in suspense or in the aftermath of an attack, heighten the sense of vulnerability and isolation. For instance, the scene where a group of soldiers hides in a beached fishing vessel, waiting for the tide to come in, is punctuated by long stretches of silence that amplify the tension and the impending sense of doom. The absence of sound in these moments forces the audience to focus more intently on the visual storytelling and the characters' expressions, making the experience more immersive and emotionally resonant. Nolan's use of silence in "Dunkirk" not only serves as a counterpoint to the action but also underscores the themes of courage, sacrifice, and the indomitable will to survive.

In "Interstellar" (2014), silence plays a crucial role in contrasting the vastness of space with the intimate human drama at the heart of the story. Space, a vacuum where sound cannot travel, is represented with eerie silence, highlighting the isolation and the unknown faced by the astronauts. One of the most impactful uses of silence occurs during a critical docking sequence, where the absence of sound intensifies the suspense and the gravity of the situation. This choice not only adheres to scientific accuracy but also serves to heighten the emotional stakes, drawing the audience deeper into the characters' perilous journey. Furthermore, the moments of silence shared between Cooper and his daughter Murph, whether through the vacuum of space or the silence of unsaid words, underscore the emotional core of the film. In these scenes, silence becomes a conduit for the unspoken bond between them, reinforcing the film's exploration of love, time, and the connections that transcend the physical universe.

Moreover, Nolan's "The Dark Knight" trilogy utilizes silence as a means to delve into the psyche of its characters, particularly Bruce Wayne/Batman. Moments of silence in these films often serve to reflect Wayne's inner turmoil and the moral ambiguities of his crusade against Gotham's underworld. Silence accompanies Bruce in the Batcave, amidst his contemplation and strategizing, serving as a stark contrast to the chaotic world above. These periods of quietude are instrumental in developing Bruce Wayne's character, allowing the audience a glimpse into the solitude and burden of his dual identity. The silence surrounding Batman also elevates his enigmatic presence, making his sudden appearances and disappearances all the more striking. In this context, silence amplifies the mythic qualities of the Batman persona, reinforcing the character's symbolic significance as a guardian shrouded in mystery and darkness.

Christopher Nolan's judicious use of silence across his filmography highlights his understanding of its power as a narrative device. By employing silence strategically, Nolan accentuates the emotional and thematic depth of his films, using it to create tension, deepen character exploration, and underscore the narrative's larger themes. Silence in Nolan's films is never merely the absence of sound but a deliberate choice that enriches the storytelling, making his cinematic works not only visually and intellectually stimulating but also emotionally profound. Through his innovative use of silence, Nolan demonstrates that true cinematic artistry lies not just in what is seen and heard but also in what is left unspoken, proving that in the hands of a master filmmaker, silence can speak volumes.

Collaboration with composers, especially Hans Zimmer: Themes and motifs.

Christopher Nolan's collaboration with composers, particularly Hans Zimmer, stands as a cornerstone of his films' emotional and thematic architecture. Their partnership, emblematic of a deep mutual understanding and creative synergy, has produced some of the most iconic scores in contemporary cinema, enriching Nolan's storytelling with musical themes and motifs that resonate deeply with audiences. Zimmer's scores for Nolan's films are not merely background music but integral components of the narrative, enhancing the films' emotional depth and amplifying their thematic concerns. In "Inception" (2010), Zimmer's score is pivotal in navigating the film's complex layers of reality and dreams. The music, with its blend of electronic and orchestral elements, mirrors the film's exploration of the subconscious, weaving a sonic tapestry that is both ethereal and grounded. The use of a slowed-down version of Edith Piaf's "Non, Je Ne Regrette Rien" as a thematic motif throughout the score exemplifies the creative use of music to underscore the film's narrative structure and emotional stakes. The motif not only serves as aural cue signaling the impending collapse of a dream layer but also resonates with the film's deeper themes of memory, regret, and the desire for redemption. Zimmer's score for "Inception" thus becomes a narrative force in its own right, guiding the audience through the film's intricacies and echoing its central questions about reality and illusion.

The collaboration between Nolan and Zimmer reached new heights with "Interstellar" (2014), where the score plays a critical role in conveying the film's grandeur and its intimate human drama. Zimmer's innovative use of the pipe organ, combined with orchestral and electronic elements, creates a sound that is vast enough to encompass the cosmos yet intimate enough to touch the heart. The organ motifs, evocative of both the majesty of space and the ticking of time, enhance the film's exploration of astrophysical phenomena and the emotional journey of its characters. The score's thematic complexity, with motifs representing love, time, and the bond between parent and child, adds layers of meaning to the narrative, making the music an essential element of the storytelling. The emotional climax of the film, underscored by Zimmer's powerful yet tender score, elevates the scene to a transcendent experience, demonstrating the profound impact of the Nolan-Zimmer collaboration on the film's narrative and thematic depth.

Furthermore, the Nolan-Zimmer partnership in "The Dark Knight" trilogy redefined the sound of superhero cinema, with Zimmer's score contributing significantly to the trilogy's dark, brooding atmosphere and its exploration of heroism and morality. The themes and motifs developed for the trilogy, such as the Joker's dissonant, unsettling theme in "The Dark Knight" (2008) or the hopeful yet melancholic theme for Batman, are masterfully crafted to reflect the characters' complexities and the trilogy's moral ambiguities. Zimmer's score, with its innovative soundscapes and emotive motifs, becomes a character in its own right, shaping the audience's perception of the narrative and deepening the emotional resonance of key moments. The music's ability to evoke the internal struggles of the characters and the external chaos of Gotham City showcases the integral role of Zimmer's compositions in Nolan's storytelling, enhancing the narrative's impact and leaving a lasting impression on the audience.

The collaborative relationship between Christopher Nolan and Hans Zimmer is a testament to the power of music in cinema, illustrating how a film's score can transcend its supporting role to become a vital part of the narrative and thematic expression. Through films like "Inception," "Interstellar," and "The Dark Knight" trilogy, Nolan and Zimmer have created aural landscapes that are as complex and compelling as the visual and narrative elements of the films themselves. Their partnership highlights the importance of collaboration in filmmaking, with Zimmer's compositions perfectly complementing

Nolan's storytelling to create cinematic experiences that are immersive, emotionally engaging, and intellectually stimulating. The themes and motifs born from this collaboration not only enhance the films in which they appear but also contribute to the larger tapestry of contemporary cinema, underscoring the enduring impact of the Nolan-Zimmer partnership on the art of film scoring.

Chapter 9: Legacy and Influence

Nolan's impact on independent and mainstream cinema.

Christopher Nolan's career trajectory, moving from independent films to becoming a titan in mainstream cinema, encapsulates his profound impact on both spheres. His journey began with "Following" (1998), a low-budget, independent film shot with a handheld camera and a minimal crew, showcasing Nolan's innovative storytelling and his ability to create compelling narratives within the constraints of independent cinema. This film, along with "Memento" (2000), demonstrated Nolan's mastery of non-linear narrative structures, a theme that has become a hallmark of his work. "Memento," in particular, with its reverse chronological order and exploration of memory and identity, not only captivated audiences but also garnered critical acclaim, signaling Nolan's potential to transform and elevate the narrative possibilities of cinema. His success in the independent film sphere challenged the conventions of storytelling, proving that audiences were ready for more complex narratives and themes, often eschewed by mainstream cinema for fear of alienating viewers. Nolan's work inspired a new generation of filmmakers to experiment with narrative structures and themes, expanding the creative boundaries of independent cinema.

Transitioning into mainstream cinema with "Batman Begins" (2005) and subsequently redefining the superhero genre with "The Dark Knight" (2008), Nolan brought the complexity and thematic depth characteristic of his independent films to a broader audience. By infusing the superhero genre with realism, moral ambiguity, and psychological depth, Nolan elevated the genre beyond its traditional confines, demonstrating that blockbuster films could possess the narrative sophistication and artistic integrity typically associated with independent cinema. This shift not only revitalized the superhero genre but also influenced mainstream cinema's approach to franchise filmmaking, paving the way for more nuanced and character-driven blockbuster films. Nolan's impact on mainstream cinema is further evidenced by his advocacy for film preservation and his use of practical effects and IMAX technology, championing the cinematic experience in an era increasingly dominated by digital filmmaking and streaming platforms. Through his work, Nolan has bridged the gap between the artistic ambitions of independent cinema and the spectacle of mainstream films, expanding the possibilities of narrative and visual storytelling across the industry.

Moreover, Nolan's engagement with complex themes such as time, memory, and identity, coupled with his innovative use of technology and narrative structures, has set new standards in filmmaking. Films like "Inception" (2010) and

"Interstellar" (2014) exemplify Nolan's ability to combine high-concept ideas with mass appeal, challenging audiences to engage intellectually while providing visually stunning and emotionally resonant cinematic experiences. This blend of intellectual rigor and mainstream accessibility has not only broadened the scope of topics explored in blockbuster films but has also encouraged a more engaged and discerning viewership. Nolan's influence extends beyond his filmography, inspiring filmmakers and studios to take creative risks and invest in original, thought-provoking content. His success has shown that there is a demand for films that challenge and entertain, reshaping industry perceptions about the commercial viability of complex narratives and themes.

Christopher Nolan's impact on both independent and mainstream cinema is indelible, marked by his commitment to narrative innovation, thematic exploration, and the cinematic experience. By seamlessly moving between independent and mainstream filmmaking, Nolan has not only expanded the narrative and visual possibilities of cinema but has also influenced the industry's approach to storytelling, technology, and audience engagement. His work has blurred the lines between art-house and blockbuster films, fostering a cinematic landscape where complexity and mass appeal are not mutually exclusive but are instead complementary forces driving the evolution of modern cinema. Nolan's legacy, characterized by his unique blend of intellectual depth and mainstream success, continues to inspire filmmakers and audiences alike, cementing his status as one of the most influential directors of his generation.

The future of filmmaking inspired by Nolan's techniques.

Christopher Nolan's impact on filmmaking and narrative construction has indelibly shaped the future of cinema, encouraging a generation of filmmakers to explore innovative storytelling techniques and embrace the artistry of the film medium. Nolan's distinctive approach—marked by non-linear narratives, practical effects, and thematic depth—has not only broadened the scope of what blockbuster films can achieve but has also redefined audience expectations. Looking forward, the influence of Nolan's techniques promises to inspire an evolution in filmmaking, where complexity and intellectual engagement become as integral to mainstream cinema as entertainment value.

Nolan's penchant for non-linear storytelling and complex narrative structures challenges both filmmakers and audiences to think beyond traditional linear narratives. This technique, evident in films like "Memento" and "Inception," has underscored the potential for cinema to explore the fluidity of time, memory, and subjective experience, encouraging filmmakers to experiment with their narrative constructions. As technology continues to advance, offering filmmakers an ever-expanding toolkit, the future of cinema will likely see an increase in films that, like Nolan's, leverage these tools not just for spectacle but for enhancing narrative depth and viewer engagement. Emerging filmmakers, inspired by Nolan, may push this envelope further, integrating virtual and augmented reality technologies to create more immersive narrative experiences that challenge the viewer's perception of story, time, and space.

Furthermore, Nolan's commitment to practical effects and shooting on film, even as digital technologies dominate, has reignited interest in these traditional techniques, highlighting their unique value in a digital age. This insistence on the tactile and the real for the sake of authenticity and viewer immersion underscores the importance of the physical medium of film and practical cinematography in creating a visually rich and emotionally engaging cinematic experience. As a result, the future of filmmaking may witness a resurgence of these traditional techniques, blending them with digital advancements to create new forms of cinematic expression that are grounded in the tangible world yet expansive in their imaginative scope.

Moreover, Nolan's thematic exploration of existential and philosophical questions within the framework of mainstream cinema has paved the way for blockbuster films that are both intellectually stimulating and widely accessible. His ability to weave complex themes with compelling narratives and character development suggests a future where cinema can be a vehicle for profound philosophical exploration without sacrificing mass appeal. This balance between depth and accessibility encourages filmmakers to tackle significant themes and encourages audiences to engage with cinema in more meaningful ways. The impact of Nolan's work suggests a future where films are recognized not only for their entertainment value but also for their capacity to provoke thought, stir debate, and reflect on the human condition.

In essence, Christopher Nolan's contributions to cinema have set a precedent for innovation, intellectual engagement, and the blending of artistry with mainstream appeal. His influence on the future of filmmaking is likely to inspire a new generation of filmmakers to explore ambitious narrative structures, integrate traditional and digital techniques, and engage with profound thematic content. As cinema continues to evolve, Nolan's legacy will remain a touchstone for those looking to push the boundaries of what film can achieve, ensuring that the future of filmmaking is as dynamic and multifaceted as the stories it seeks to tell. Through the inspiration drawn from Nolan's techniques, the future of cinema promises to be an exciting fusion of technology, narrative innovation, and deep thematic exploration.

Appendix

Filmography of Christopher Nolan.

1. Following (1998): Nolan's debut feature film, "Following," is a noir-inspired thriller that explores themes of obsession, voyeurism, and deception. The story revolves around a young, unnamed writer who begins following strangers around London, seeking inspiration for his characters. This curiosity leads him into the world of a charismatic thief, pulling him deeper into a criminal underworld than he anticipated. The film is noted for its non-linear narrative and black-and-white cinematography, showcasing Nolan's early interest in complex storytelling and psychological depth.

2. Memento (2000): This groundbreaking narrative employs a unique reverse chronological order to immerse viewers in the fragmented and unreliable memory of Leonard Shelby, a man determined to find his wife's murderer despite his short-term memory loss. "Memento" challenges conventional storytelling and explores themes of identity, reality, and the fallibility of memory, cementing Nolan's reputation as a filmmaker who combines narrative innovation with deep thematic exploration.

3. Insomnia (2002): In this psychological thriller, two LAPD detectives are sent to a small Alaskan town to investigate the murder of a teenage girl. The film delves into the moral ambiguities of justice and redemption, as Detective Will Dormer (played by Al Pacino) grapples with guilt, sleeplessness, and an adversary who challenges his ethical boundaries. "Insomnia" showcases Nolan's skill in creating tension-filled atmospheres and complex characters.

4. Batman Begins (2005): This film reimagines the origin story of Batman, delving into Bruce Wayne's transformation into the Dark Knight and his battle against crime and corruption in Gotham City. "Batman Begins" marks Nolan's foray into blockbuster filmmaking, blending action, psychological depth, and a realistic approach to the superhero genre. The film explores themes of fear, justice, and identity, setting the tone for the subsequent films in The Dark Knight Trilogy.

5. The Prestige (2006): Set in the world of Victorian-era magicians, "The Prestige" is a tale of obsession, sacrifice, and the art of illusion. The rivalry between two magicians becomes a deadly battle of wits and deception, leading to tragic consequences. The film is noted for its intricate plot, thematic complexity, and the exploration of the costs of ambition and obsession.

6. The Dark Knight (2008): The second installment in The Dark Knight Trilogy, "The Dark Knight," is widely regarded as one of the greatest superhero films of all time. It pits Batman against his anarchic nemesis, the Joker, in a battle for Gotham's soul. The film explores themes of chaos, morality, and the thin line between heroism and vigilantism, bolstered by Heath Ledger's iconic performance as the Joker.

7. Inception (2010): This sci-fi thriller explores the world of dream infiltration and the possibility of planting ideas into someone's subconscious. "Inception" is celebrated for its original concept, stunning visuals, and the intellectual challenge it poses to its audience, delving into themes of reality, loss, and redemption.

8. The Dark Knight Rises (2012): The final chapter of The Dark Knight Trilogy, "The Dark Knight Rises," sees Batman confronting the physical and ideological force of Bane, a new villain intent on destroying Gotham. The film examines themes of resilience, redemption, and legacy, concluding Bruce Wayne's journey as Batman in an epic narrative of struggle and sacrifice.

9. Interstellar (2014): A visually spectacular exploration of space travel, time dilation, and the human spirit, "Interstellar" follows a group of astronauts on a mission to find humanity a new home. The film combines emotional depth with scientific concepts, probing the limits of human endeavor and the bonds of love across time and space.

10. Dunkirk (2017): This World War II epic presents the Dunkirk evacuation from three perspectives: land, sea, and air. "Dunkirk" is noted for its minimal dialogue, intense realism, and innovative storytelling structure, offering a visceral, immersive experience of war and survival.

11. Oppenheimer (2023): During World War II, Lt. Gen. Leslie Groves Jr. appoints physicist J. Robert Oppenheimer to work on the top-secret Manhattan Project. Oppenheimer and a team of scientists spend years developing and designing the atomic bomb. Their work comes to fruition on July 16, 1945, as they witness the world's first nuclear explosion, forever changing the course of history.

10 films to watch that inspired Nolan.

Christopher Nolan, known for his innovative storytelling and technical prowess, draws inspiration from a diverse array of films. Here are ten films that have inspired him, offering insights into the elements that influence his unique filmmaking style:

1. 2001: A Space Odyssey (1968, Stanley Kubrick): A cornerstone of science fiction cinema, Kubrick's masterpiece is renowned for its groundbreaking visuals, profound narrative depth, and pioneering depiction of space travel. Nolan has cited it as a significant influence, especially evident in his own space exploration epic, "Interstellar."

2. Blade Runner (1982, Ridley Scott): This seminal work of neo-noir science fiction, with its themes of identity, consciousness, and the nature of humanity, has left a lasting impact on Nolan. The film's visual style and complex storytelling echo through Nolan's work, particularly in his portrayal of morally ambiguous characters and dystopian settings.

3. The Thin Red Line (1998, Terrence Malick): Malick's meditative war film, known for its philosophical introspection and stunning cinematography, has influenced Nolan's approach to the existential themes and visual presentation in his films, such as "Dunkirk."

4. Heat (1995, Michael Mann): Nolan has often expressed his admiration for Mann's crime saga, particularly its intricate plot, character development, and the iconic Los Angeles backdrop. The influence of "Heat" is evident in Nolan's "The Dark Knight," especially in its portrayal of the cat-and-mouse dynamic between Batman and the Joker.

5. A Clockwork Orange (1971, Stanley Kubrick): Kubrick's controversial masterpiece, with its exploration of free will, violence, and societal control, has impacted Nolan's thematic interests, particularly in exploring the darker aspects of human nature and the ethical dilemmas faced by his characters.

6. 12 Angry Men (1957, Sidney Lumet): This classic courtroom drama, centered on a jury's deliberations, showcases the power of dialogue and character-driven storytelling. Nolan admires Lumet's ability to create tension and drama within a confined space, a technique Nolan has employed in films like "The Prestige."

7. Vertigo (1958, Alfred Hitchcock): Hitchcock's psychological thriller, with its innovative use of camera techniques and exploration of obsession, has been a source of inspiration for Nolan. Themes of identity, obsession, and the blurring of reality and illusion in Nolan's work can be traced back to "Vertigo."

8. Metropolis (1927, Fritz Lang): Lang's pioneering science fiction epic, with its depiction of a dystopian future and the struggle between different social classes, has influenced Nolan's interest in societal themes and the use of architecture and urban environments in his films.

9. Lawrence of Arabia (1962, David Lean): Lean's epic biographical film is celebrated for its grand scale, sweeping landscapes, and complex portrayal of T.E. Lawrence. Nolan admires Lean's ability to combine epic storytelling with deep character exploration, an approach Nolan aspires to in his own epics.

10. The Man Who Would Be King (1975, John Huston): This adventure film, based on Rudyard Kipling's novella, is known for its themes of friendship, imperialism, and the corrupting nature of power. Nolan has cited it as an influence, drawn to its epic tale of adventure and moral complexity.

These films, spanning genres and decades, provide a window into the cinematic influences that have shaped Christopher Nolan's approach to filmmaking, from narrative complexity and thematic depth to visual style and character development.

Glossary of film terms.

1. Aspect Ratio: The proportional relationship between a film's width and height. It significantly affects the composition and visual impact of each shot. Nolan often utilizes the IMAX aspect ratio for its high resolution and immersive quality.

2. Blocking: The precise staging of actors and the camera's movement within a scene. Effective blocking is crucial for visual storytelling, guiding the audience's focus and enhancing the narrative through physical positioning and movement.

3. Cross-Cutting: An editing technique that alternates between two or more scenes happening simultaneously, used to build suspense or show parallel narratives.

4. Diegetic Sound: Sound that originates from the story world, including characters' dialogue, sounds made by objects in the scene, and music coming from instruments within the story.

5. Dolly Shot: A shot where the camera is mounted on a wheeled platform that moves along tracks for smooth movement. It can follow a character or move through a space to enhance the narrative depth.

6. Jump Cut: An abrupt transition between two shots, either of the same subject or different ones, which can show a rapid change in time or convey a disjointed feeling.

7. Montage: A sequence of shots edited together to condense space, time, and information, often used to show the passage of time or a series of actions leading to a particular result.

8. Non-Diegetic Sound: Sound that is not part of the story world and is intended only for the audience, including the film's score, sound effects added for emphasis, and voiceover narration.

9. Non-Linear Narrative: A storytelling technique that presents the story out of chronological order, using flashbacks, flash-forwards, or a fragmented sequence of events to tell the story.

10. Practical Effects: Physical effects produced without computer-generated imagery or digital enhancement, used to create real, tangible elements on set, such as explosions, makeup effects, and mechanical props.

11. Pre-visualization (Previs): The process of visualizing complex scenes in a movie before filming, using computer graphics and animation tools to create a rough draft of a sequence or scene.